PERSEUS

THE HUNT FOR MEDUSA'S HEAD

A GREEK MYTH

GRAPHIC UNIVERSE™

STORY BY
PAUL D. STORRIE
PENCILS AND INKS BY
THOMAS YEATES

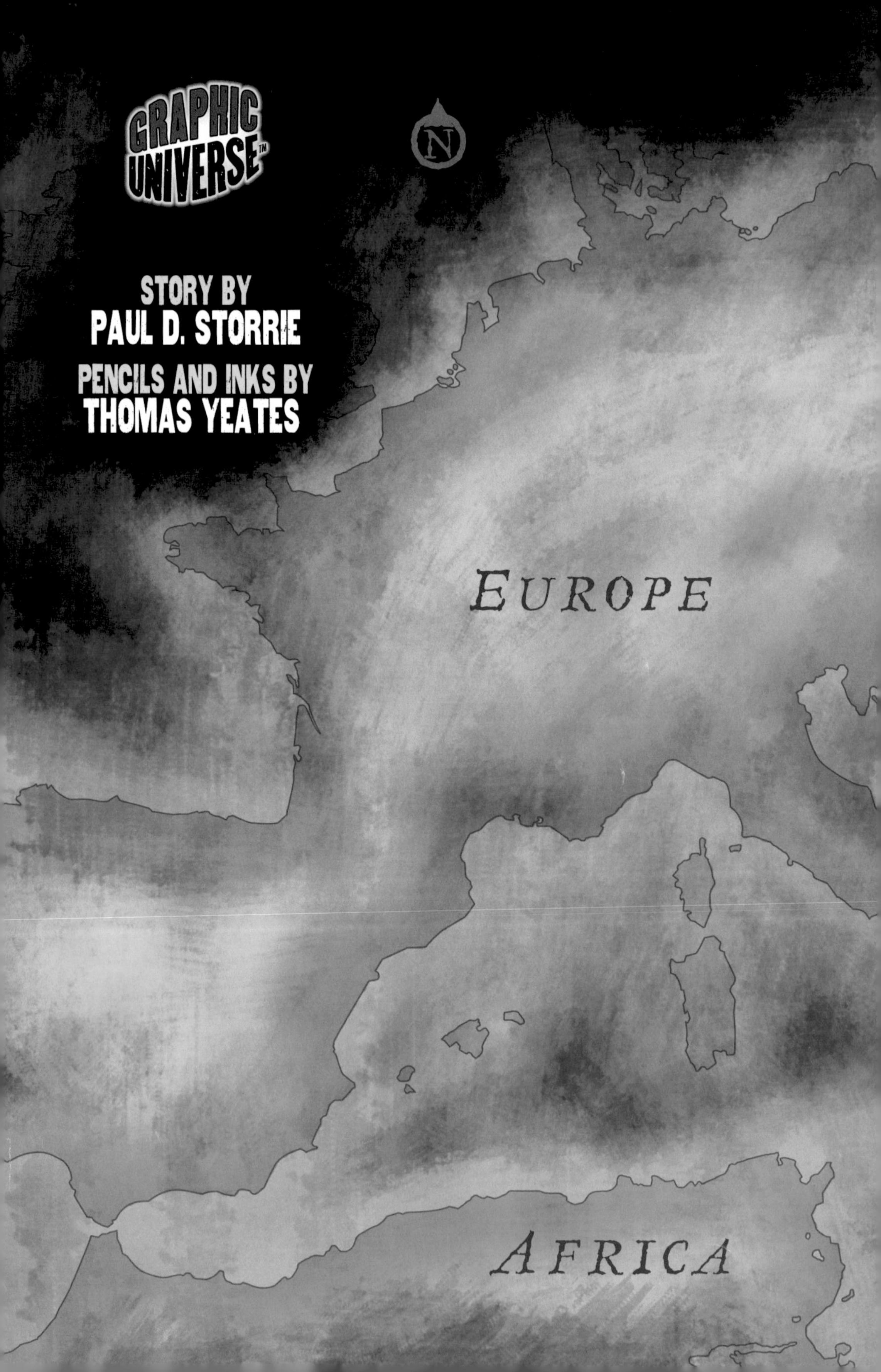
N
EUROPE
AFRICA

PERSEUS

THE HUNT FOR MEDUSA'S HEAD

A GREEK MYTH

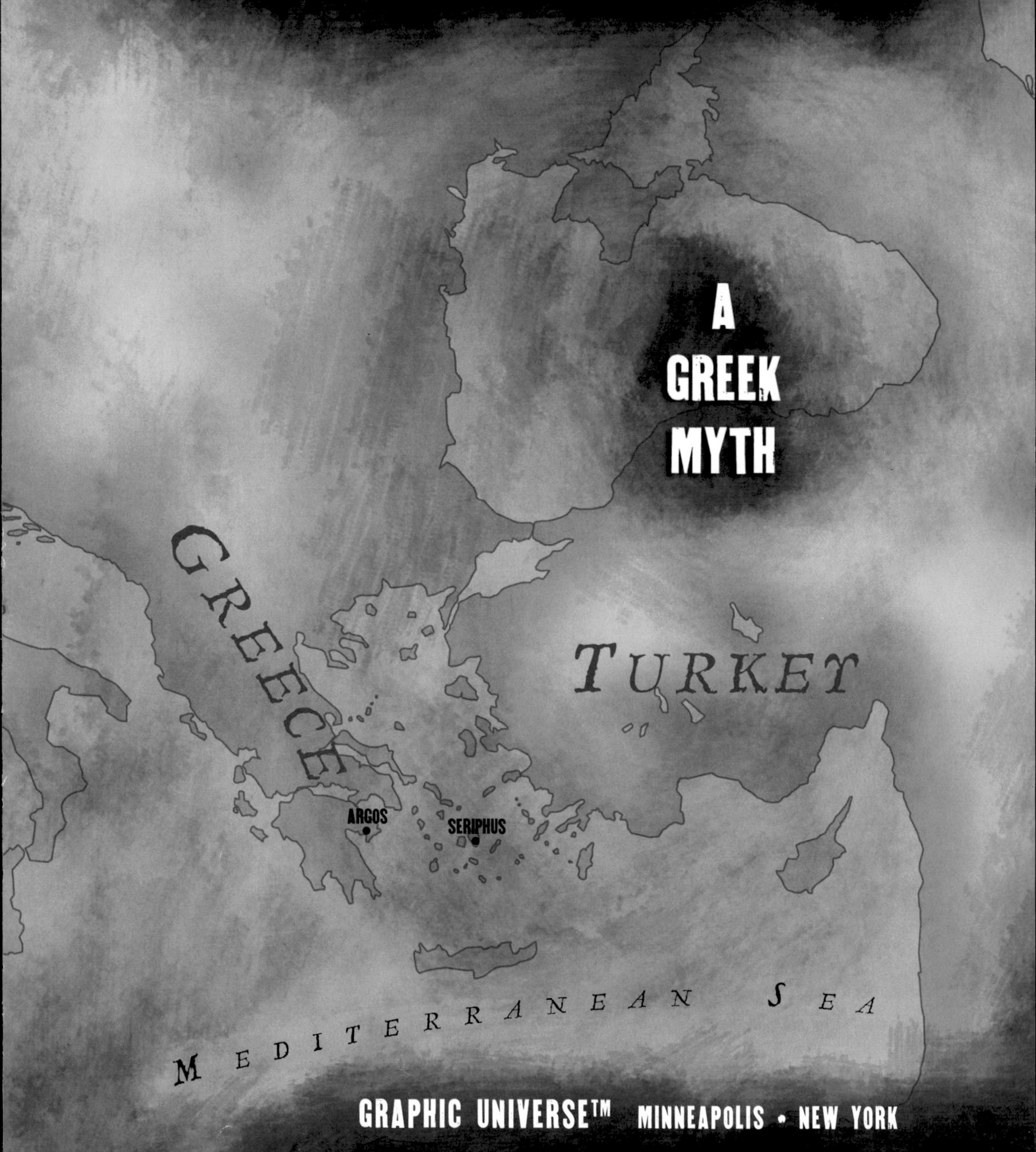
GREECE
TURKEY
ARGOS
SERIPHUS
MEDITERRANEAN SEA

GRAPHIC UNIVERSE™ MINNEAPOLIS • NEW YORK

Perseus is one of the greatest heroes of Greek literature. The legendary feats of Zeus' son have been passed down from generation to generation for more than two thousand years. To create the Graphic Myths and Legends version of Perseus' story, author Paul Storrie relied heavily on both Thomas Bulfinch's The Age of Fable, first published in 1859, and Edith Hamilton's Mythology, first published in 1942. Both of these well-known works drew their material from the writings of the ancient poets such as Ovid and Virgil. Artist Thomas Yeates consulted numerous historical and traditional sources to give the art an authentic feel, from classical Greek architecture to the clothing, weapons, and armor worn by the characters. Professor David Mulroy of the University of Wisconsin-Milwaukee ensured historical and visual accuracy.

STORY BY PAUL D. STORRIE

PENCILS AND INKS BY THOMAS YEATES
WITH TOD SMITH AND KEN HOOPER

COLORING BY HI-FI COLOUR DESIGN

LETTERING BY INTERFACE GRAPHICS, INC.

CONSULTANT: DAVID MULROY, PhD.
UNIVERSITY OF WISCONSIN—MILWAUKEE

Graphic Universe™
A division of Lerner Publishing Group, Inc.
241 First Avenue North
Minneapolis, MN 55401 U.S.A.

Website: www.lernerbooks.com

Library of Congress Cataloging-in-Publication Data

Storrie, Paul D.
    Perseus : the hunt for Medusa's head : a Greek myth /
    Story by Paul D. Storrie ; pencils and inks by Thomas Yeates.
        p. cm. — (Graphic myths and legends)
    Includes index.
    ISBN-13: 978-0-8225-7528-3 (lib. bdg. : alk. paper)
    1. Perseus (Greek mythology)—Juvenile literature.
    2. Perseus (Greek mythology)—Comic books, strips, etc. I. Yeates, Thomas. II. Title.
    BL820.P5S76 2008
    741.5'973—dc22   2007025695

Manufactured in the United States of America
1 2 3 4 5 6 - JR - 13 12 11 10 09 08

TABLE OF CONTENTS

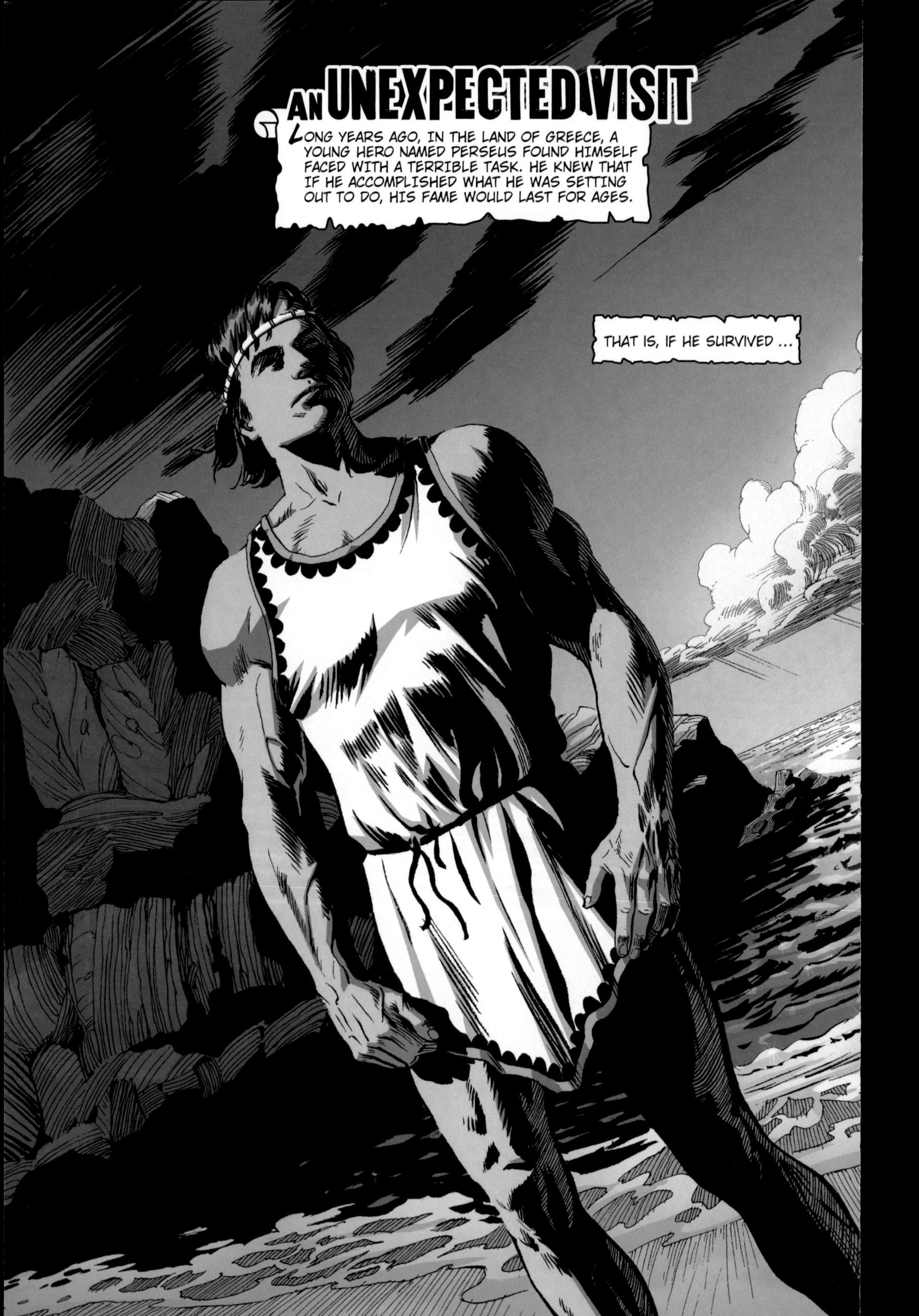
AN UNEXPECTED VISIT
LONG YEARS AGO, IN THE LAND OF GREECE, A YOUNG HERO NAMED PERSEUS FOUND HIMSELF FACED WITH A TERRIBLE TASK. HE KNEW THAT IF HE ACCOMPLISHED WHAT HE WAS SETTING OUT TO DO, HIS FAME WOULD LAST FOR AGES.
THAT IS, IF HE SURVIVED ...

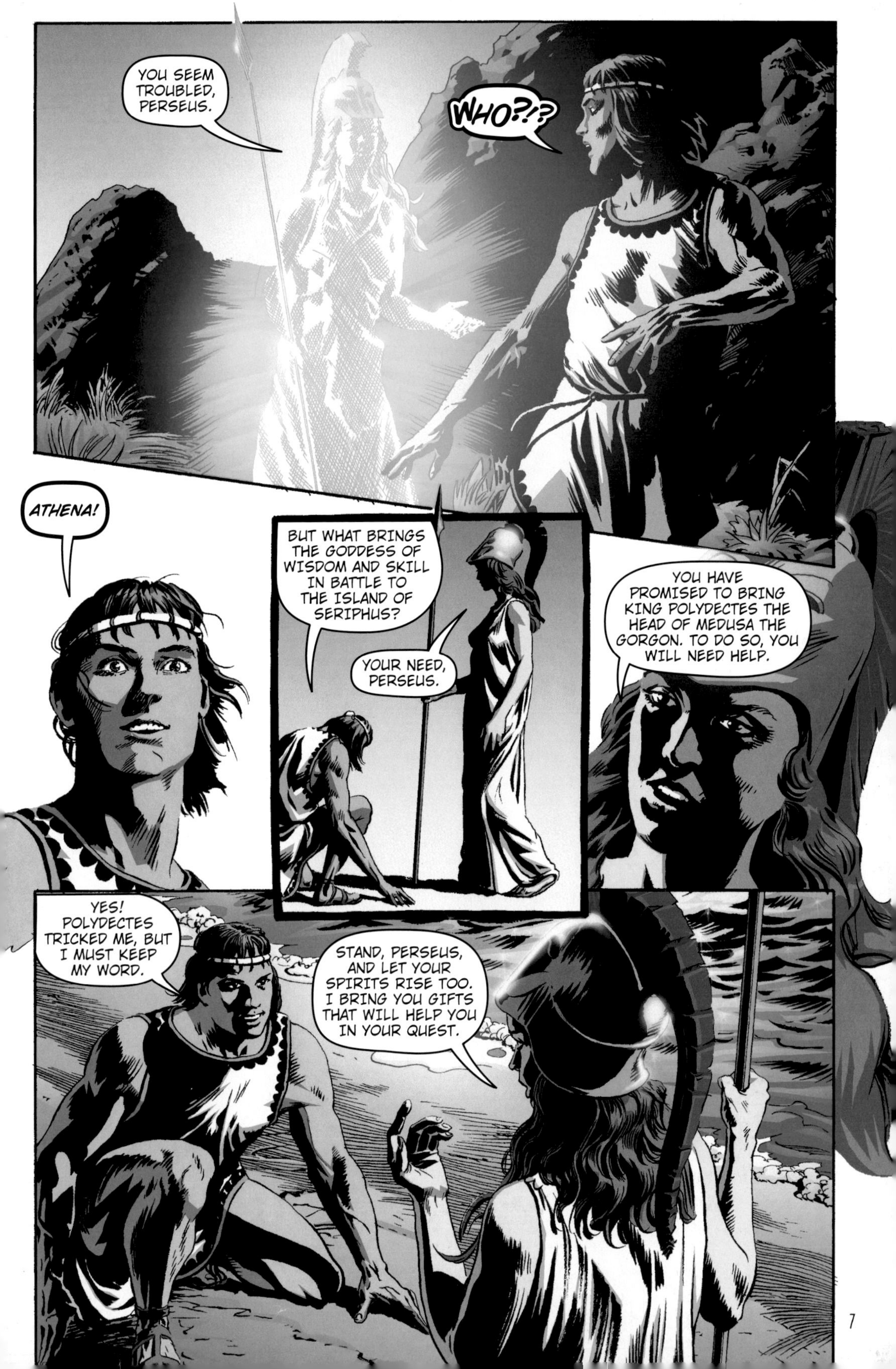
YOU SEEM TROUBLED, PERSEUS.
WHO?!?
ATHENA!
BUT WHAT BRINGS THE GODDESS OF WISDOM AND SKILL IN BATTLE TO THE ISLAND OF SERIPHUS?
YOUR NEED, PERSEUS.
YOU HAVE PROMISED TO BRING KING POLYDECTES THE HEAD OF MEDUSA THE GORGON. TO DO SO, YOU WILL NEED HELP.
YES! POLYDECTES TRICKED ME, BUT I MUST KEEP MY WORD.
STAND, PERSEUS, AND LET YOUR SPIRITS RISE TOO. I BRING YOU GIFTS THAT WILL HELP YOU IN YOUR QUEST.

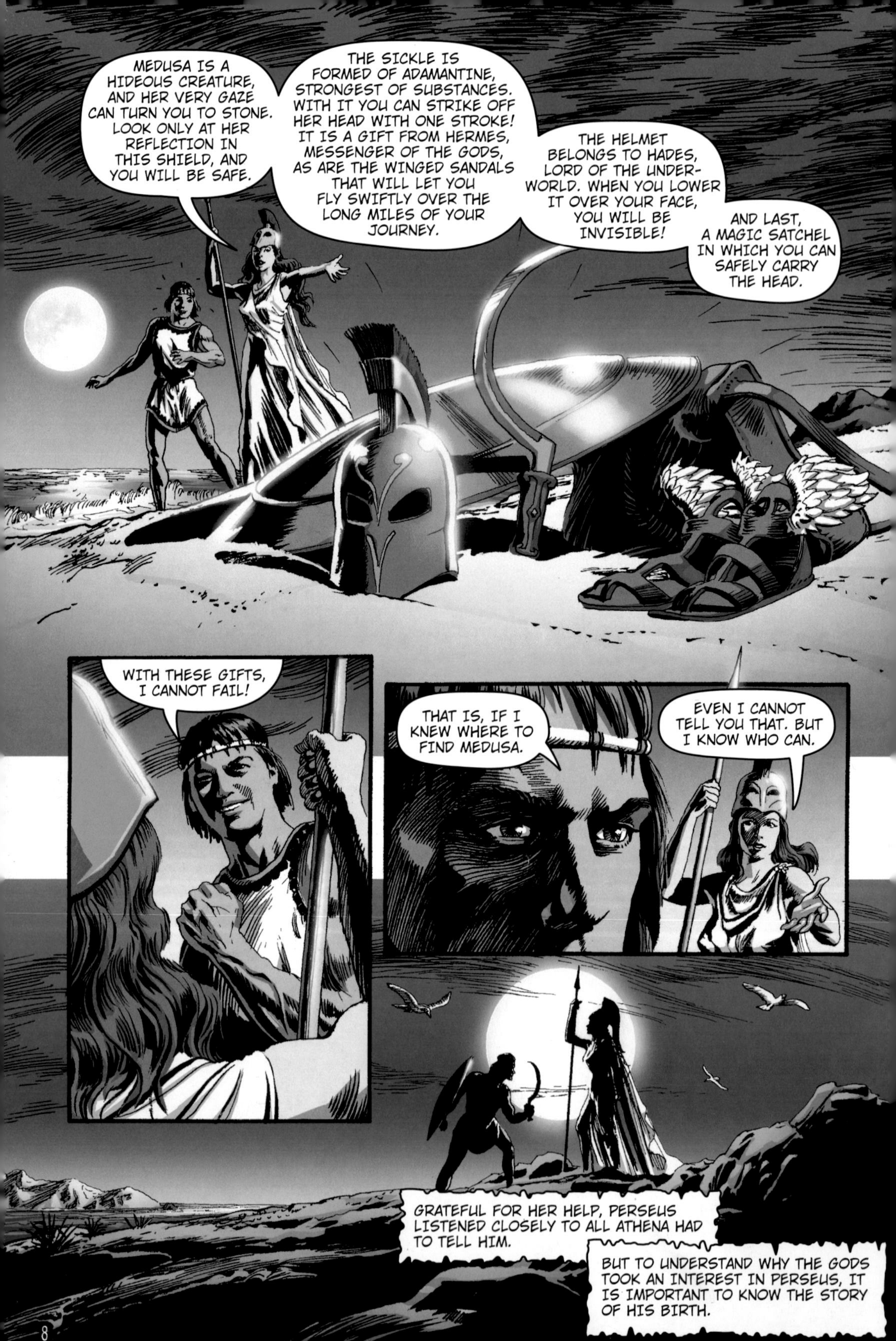
MEDUSA IS A HIDEOUS CREATURE, AND HER VERY GAZE CAN TURN YOU TO STONE. LOOK ONLY AT HER REFLECTION IN THIS SHIELD, AND YOU WILL BE SAFE.
THE SICKLE IS FORMED OF ADAMANTINE, STRONGEST OF SUBSTANCES. WITH IT YOU CAN STRIKE OFF HER HEAD WITH ONE STROKE! IT IS A GIFT FROM HERMES, MESSENGER OF THE GODS, AS ARE THE WINGED SANDALS THAT WILL LET YOU FLY SWIFTLY OVER THE LONG MILES OF YOUR JOURNEY.
THE HELMET BELONGS TO HADES, LORD OF THE UNDER-WORLD. WHEN YOU LOWER IT OVER YOUR FACE, YOU WILL BE INVISIBLE!
AND LAST, A MAGIC SATCHEL IN WHICH YOU CAN SAFELY CARRY THE HEAD.
WITH THESE GIFTS, I CANNOT FAIL!
THAT IS, IF I KNEW WHERE TO FIND MEDUSA.
EVEN I CANNOT TELL YOU THAT. BUT I KNOW WHO CAN.
GRATEFUL FOR HER HELP, PERSEUS LISTENED CLOSELY TO ALL ATHENA HAD TO TELL HIM.
BUT TO UNDERSTAND WHY THE GODS TOOK AN INTEREST IN PERSEUS, IT IS IMPORTANT TO KNOW THE STORY OF HIS BIRTH.

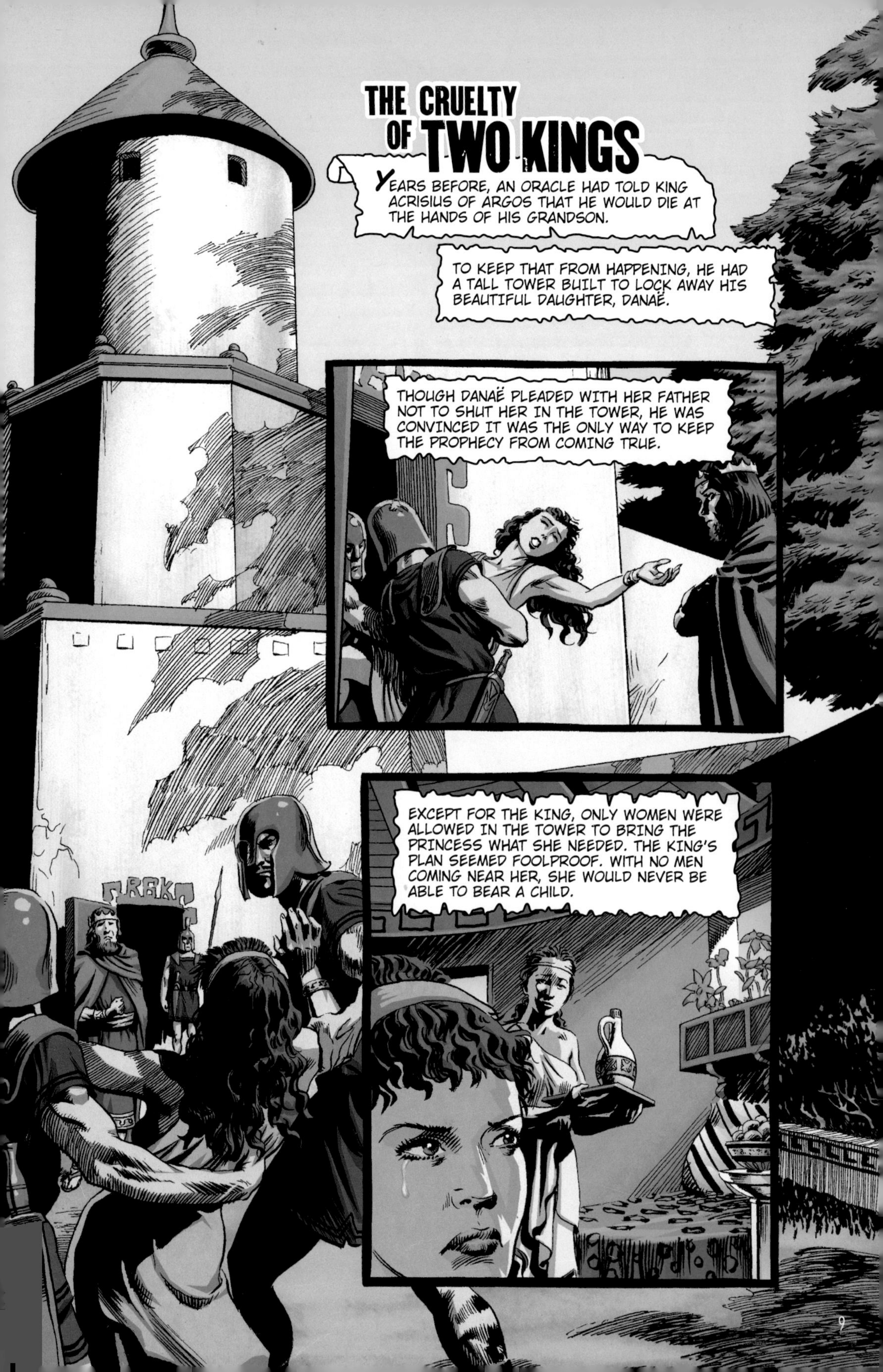
THE CRUELTY OF TWO KINGS
YEARS BEFORE, AN ORACLE HAD TOLD KING ACRISIUS OF ARGOS THAT HE WOULD DIE AT THE HANDS OF HIS GRANDSON.
TO KEEP THAT FROM HAPPENING, HE HAD A TALL TOWER BUILT TO LOCK AWAY HIS BEAUTIFUL DAUGHTER, DANAË.
THOUGH DANAË PLEADED WITH HER FATHER NOT TO SHUT HER IN THE TOWER, HE WAS CONVINCED IT WAS THE ONLY WAY TO KEEP THE PROPHECY FROM COMING TRUE.
EXCEPT FOR THE KING, ONLY WOMEN WERE ALLOWED IN THE TOWER TO BRING THE PRINCESS WHAT SHE NEEDED. THE KING'S PLAN SEEMED FOOLPROOF. WITH NO MEN COMING NEAR HER, SHE WOULD NEVER BE ABLE TO BEAR A CHILD.

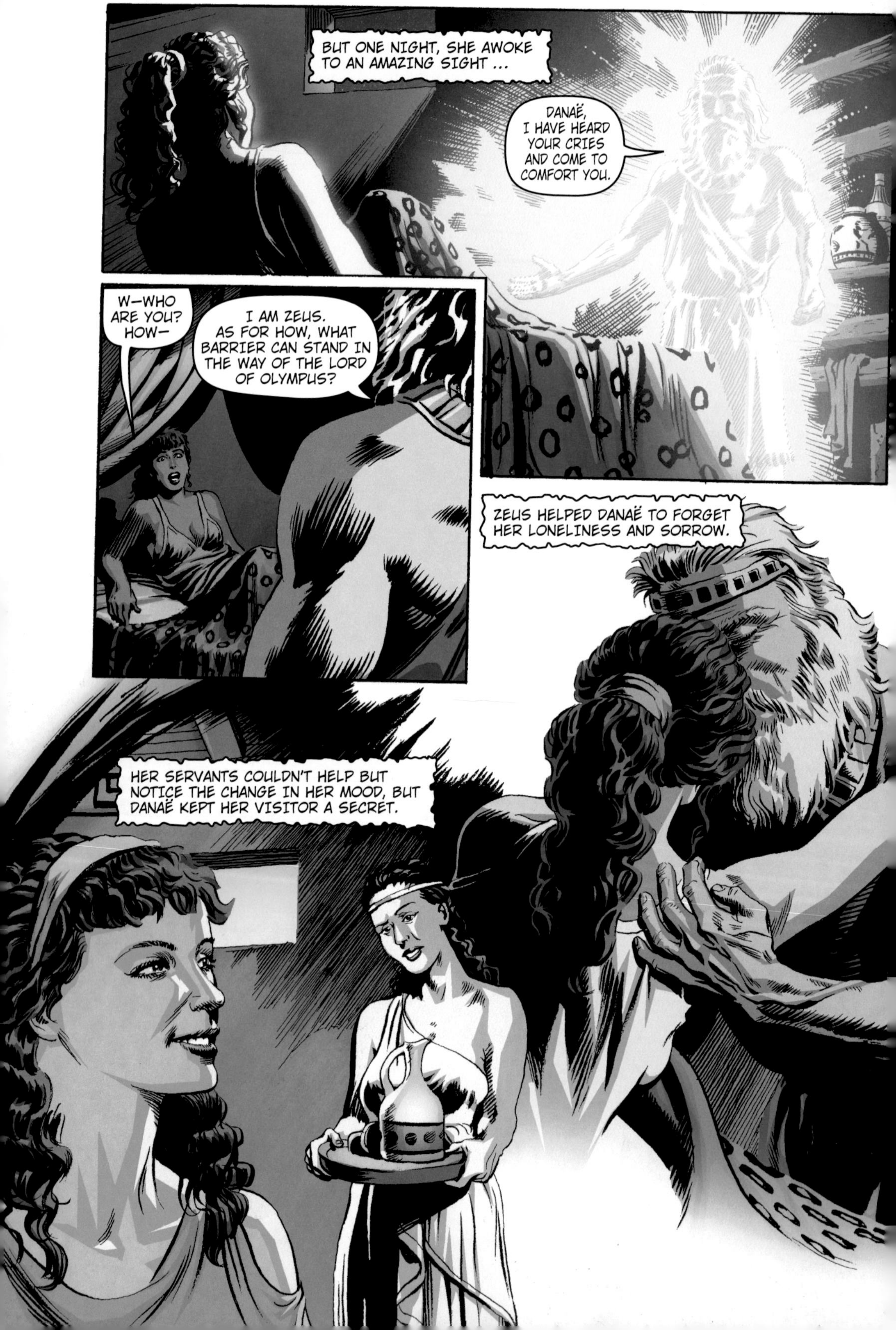

BUT ONE NIGHT, SHE AWOKE TO AN AMAZING SIGHT ...
DANAË, I HAVE HEARD YOUR CRIES AND COME TO COMFORT YOU.
W—WHO ARE YOU? HOW—
I AM ZEUS. AS FOR HOW, WHAT BARRIER CAN STAND IN THE WAY OF THE LORD OF OLYMPUS?
ZEUS HELPED DANAË TO FORGET HER LONELINESS AND SORROW.
HER SERVANTS COULDN'T HELP BUT NOTICE THE CHANGE IN HER MOOD, BUT DANAË KEPT HER VISITOR A SECRET.

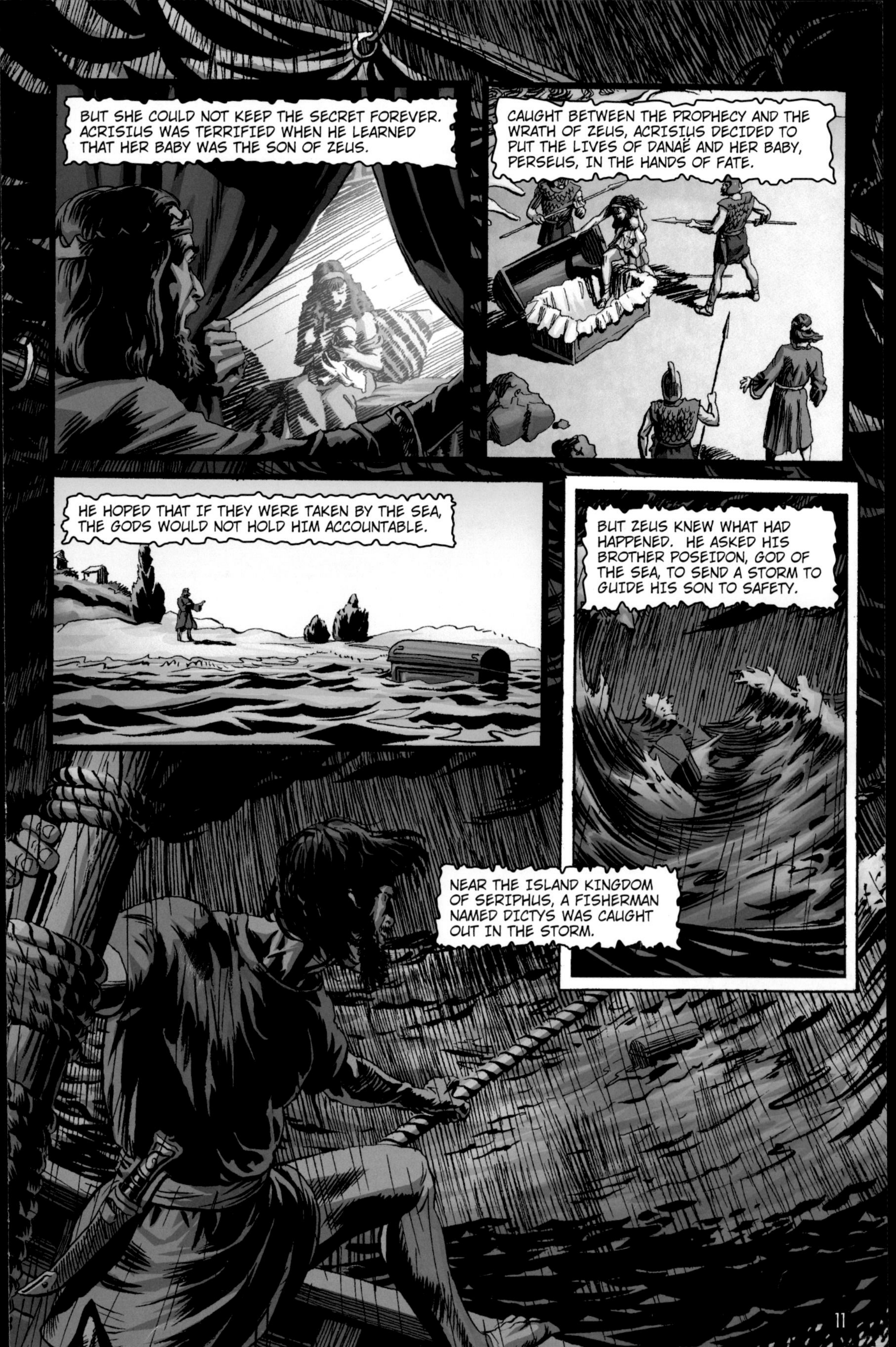
BUT SHE COULD NOT KEEP THE SECRET FOREVER. ACRISIUS WAS TERRIFIED WHEN HE LEARNED THAT HER BABY WAS THE SON OF ZEUS.
CAUGHT BETWEEN THE PROPHECY AND THE WRATH OF ZEUS, ACRISIUS DECIDED TO PUT THE LIVES OF DANAË AND HER BABY, PERSEUS, IN THE HANDS OF FATE.
HE HOPED THAT IF THEY WERE TAKEN BY THE SEA, THE GODS WOULD NOT HOLD HIM ACCOUNTABLE.
BUT ZEUS KNEW WHAT HAD HAPPENED. HE ASKED HIS BROTHER POSEIDON, GOD OF THE SEA, TO SEND A STORM TO GUIDE HIS SON TO SAFETY.
NEAR THE ISLAND KINGDOM OF SERIPHUS, A FISHERMAN NAMED DICTYS WAS CAUGHT OUT IN THE STORM.

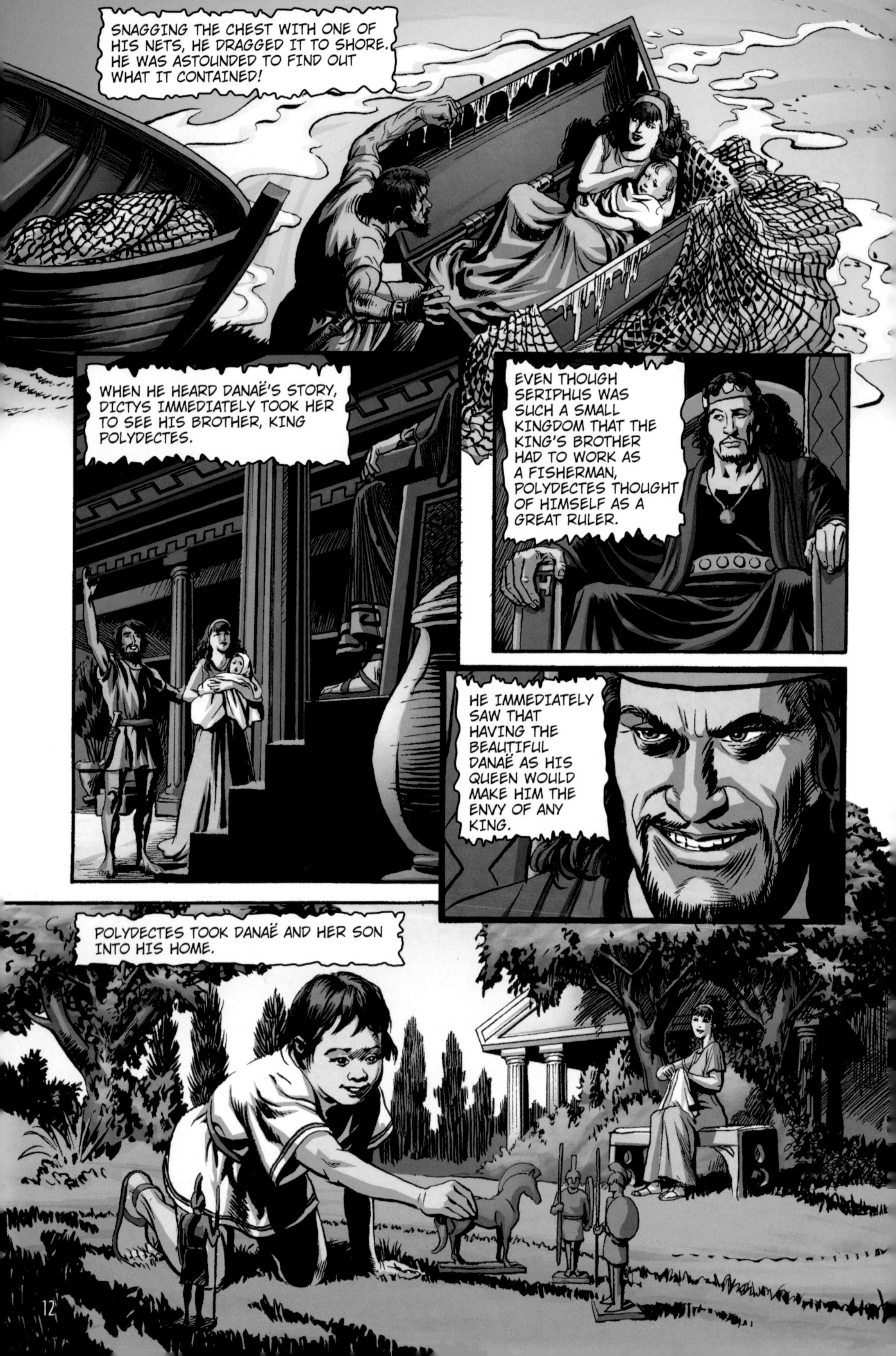
SNAGGING THE CHEST WITH ONE OF HIS NETS, HE DRAGGED IT TO SHORE. HE WAS ASTOUNDED TO FIND OUT WHAT IT CONTAINED!
WHEN HE HEARD DANAË'S STORY, DICTYS IMMEDIATELY TOOK HER TO SEE HIS BROTHER, KING POLYDECTES.
EVEN THOUGH SERIPHUS WAS SUCH A SMALL KINGDOM THAT THE KING'S BROTHER HAD TO WORK AS A FISHERMAN, POLYDECTES THOUGHT OF HIMSELF AS A GREAT RULER.
HE IMMEDIATELY SAW THAT HAVING THE BEAUTIFUL DANAË AS HIS QUEEN WOULD MAKE HIM THE ENVY OF ANY KING.
POLYDECTES TOOK DANAË AND HER SON INTO HIS HOME.

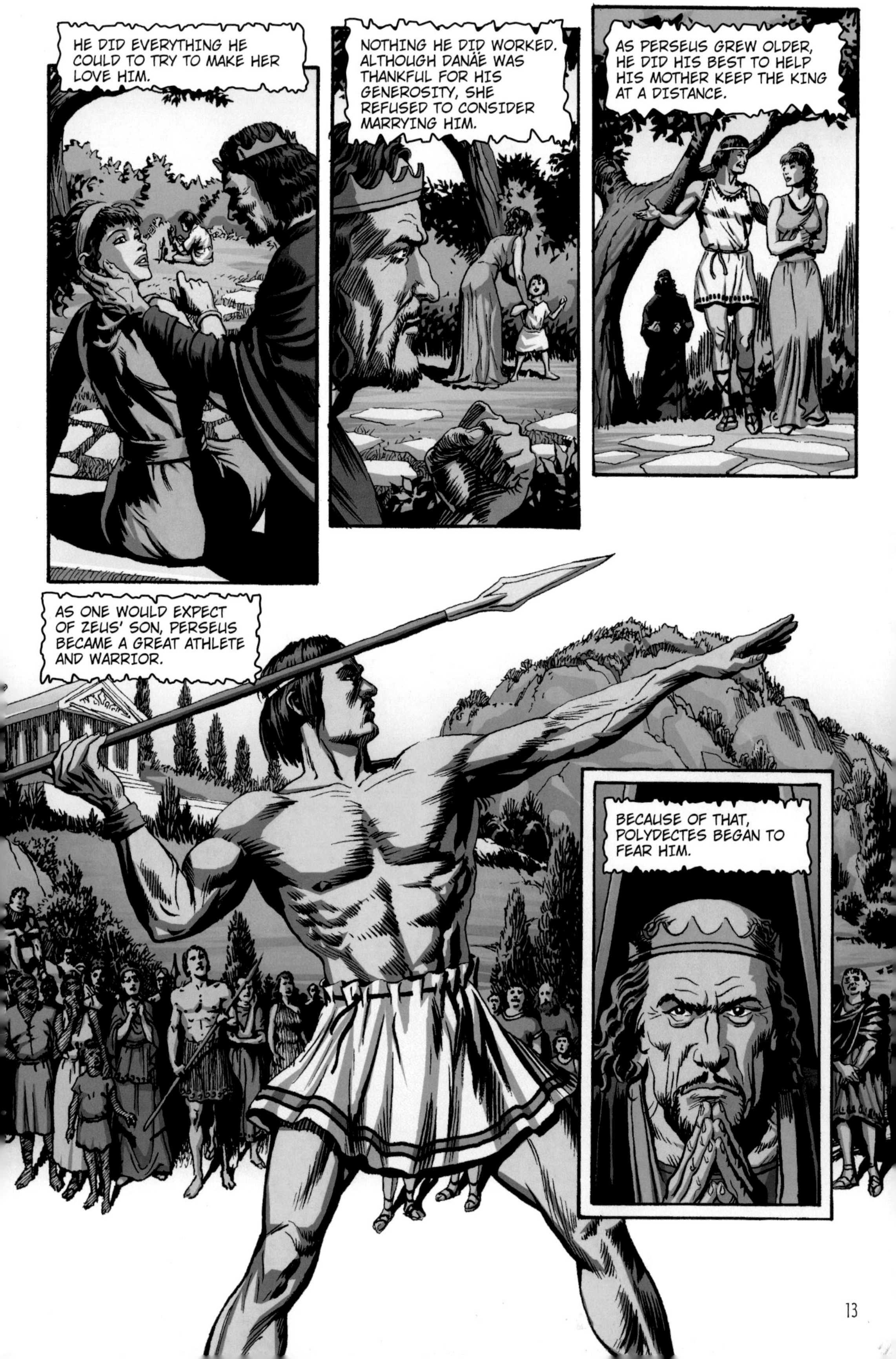
HE DID EVERYTHING HE COULD TO TRY TO MAKE HER LOVE HIM.
NOTHING HE DID WORKED. ALTHOUGH DANÄE WAS THANKFUL FOR HIS GENEROSITY, SHE REFUSED TO CONSIDER MARRYING HIM.
AS PERSEUS GREW OLDER, HE DID HIS BEST TO HELP HIS MOTHER KEEP THE KING AT A DISTANCE.
AS ONE WOULD EXPECT OF ZEUS' SON, PERSEUS BECAME A GREAT ATHLETE AND WARRIOR.
BECAUSE OF THAT, POLYDECTES BEGAN TO FEAR HIM.

BUT POLYDECTES WAS CUNNING. HE CAME UP WITH A PLAN TO GET RID OF PERSEUS. THAT WAY DANAË WOULD HAVE TO RELY UPON THE KING FOR STRENGTH AND PROTECTION.

SINCE YOUR MOTHER STILL DOES NOT WISH TO MARRY ME, I HAVE DECIDED TO PROPOSE TO HIPPODAMIA, THE DAUGHTER OF KING PELOPS.

THAT'S WONDERFUL! I HOPE THE TWO OF YOU WILL BE HAPPY TOGETHER.

IT'S NOT SO SIMPLE, PERSEUS. PELOPS RULES A GREAT LAND. MANY KINGS WISH TO MARRY HIS DAUGHTER.

ALL THE MEN OF SERIPHUS HAVE GIVEN ME FINE HORSES TO PRESEN[T] AS A GIFT TO PRO[VE] TO HIPPODAMIA AN[D] HER FATHER THAT I AND MY KINGDOM ARE WORTHY.

I HAVE NO HORSES TO GIVE, BUT ASK ME FOR ANYTHING, AND I PROMISE THAT I WILL GET IT FOR YOU!

ANYTHING?

14

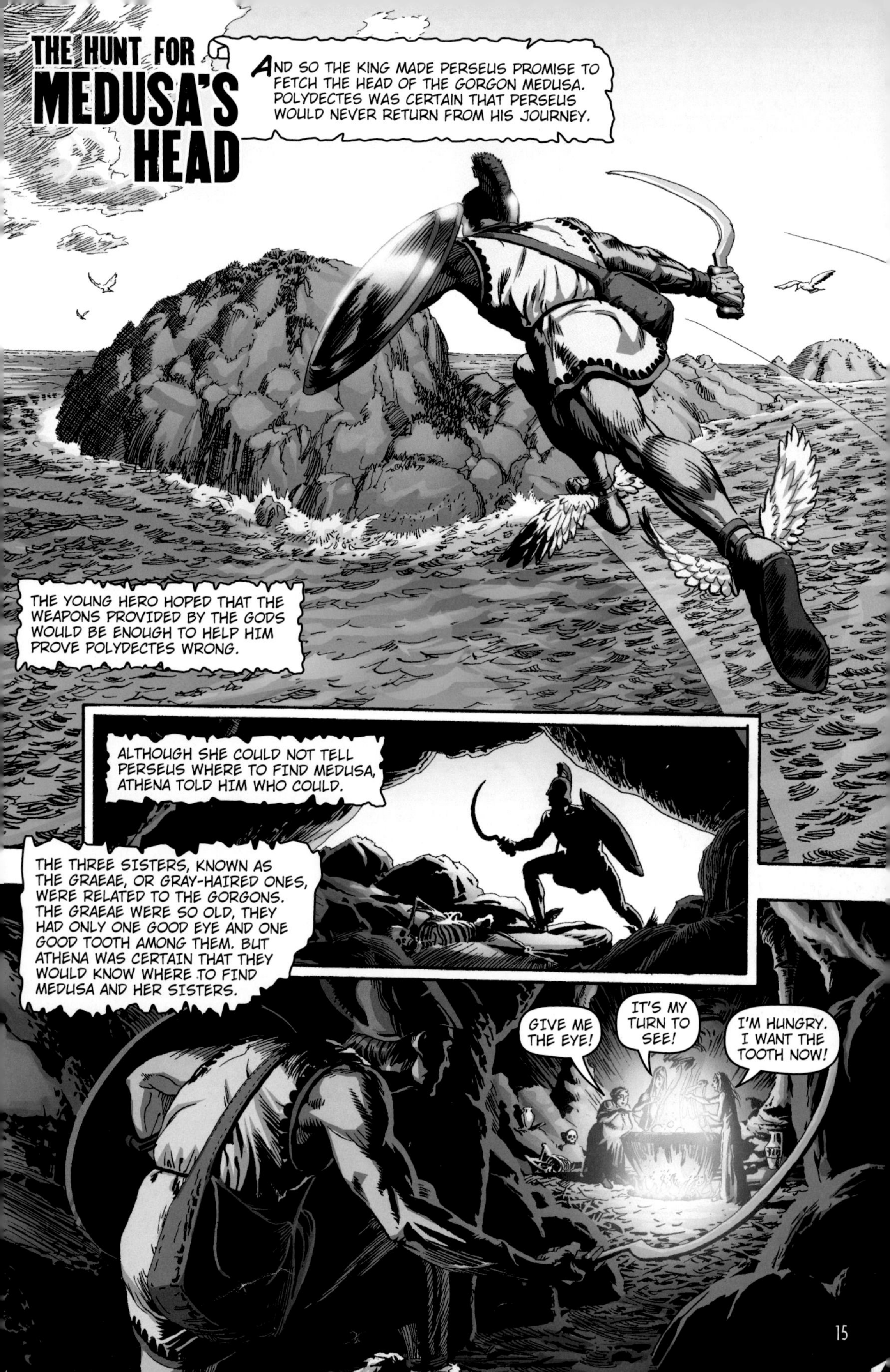
THE HUNT FOR MEDUSA'S HEAD
AND SO THE KING MADE PERSEUS PROMISE TO FETCH THE HEAD OF THE GORGON MEDUSA. POLYDECTES WAS CERTAIN THAT PERSEUS WOULD NEVER RETURN FROM HIS JOURNEY.
THE YOUNG HERO HOPED THAT THE WEAPONS PROVIDED BY THE GODS WOULD BE ENOUGH TO HELP HIM PROVE POLYDECTES WRONG.
ALTHOUGH SHE COULD NOT TELL PERSEUS WHERE TO FIND MEDUSA, ATHENA TOLD HIM WHO COULD.
THE THREE SISTERS, KNOWN AS THE GRAEAE, OR GRAY-HAIRED ONES, WERE RELATED TO THE GORGONS. THE GRAEAE WERE SO OLD, THEY HAD ONLY ONE GOOD EYE AND ONE GOOD TOOTH AMONG THEM. BUT ATHENA WAS CERTAIN THAT THEY WOULD KNOW WHERE TO FIND MEDUSA AND HER SISTERS.
GIVE ME THE EYE!
IT'S MY TURN TO SEE!
I'M HUNGRY. I WANT THE TOOTH NOW!

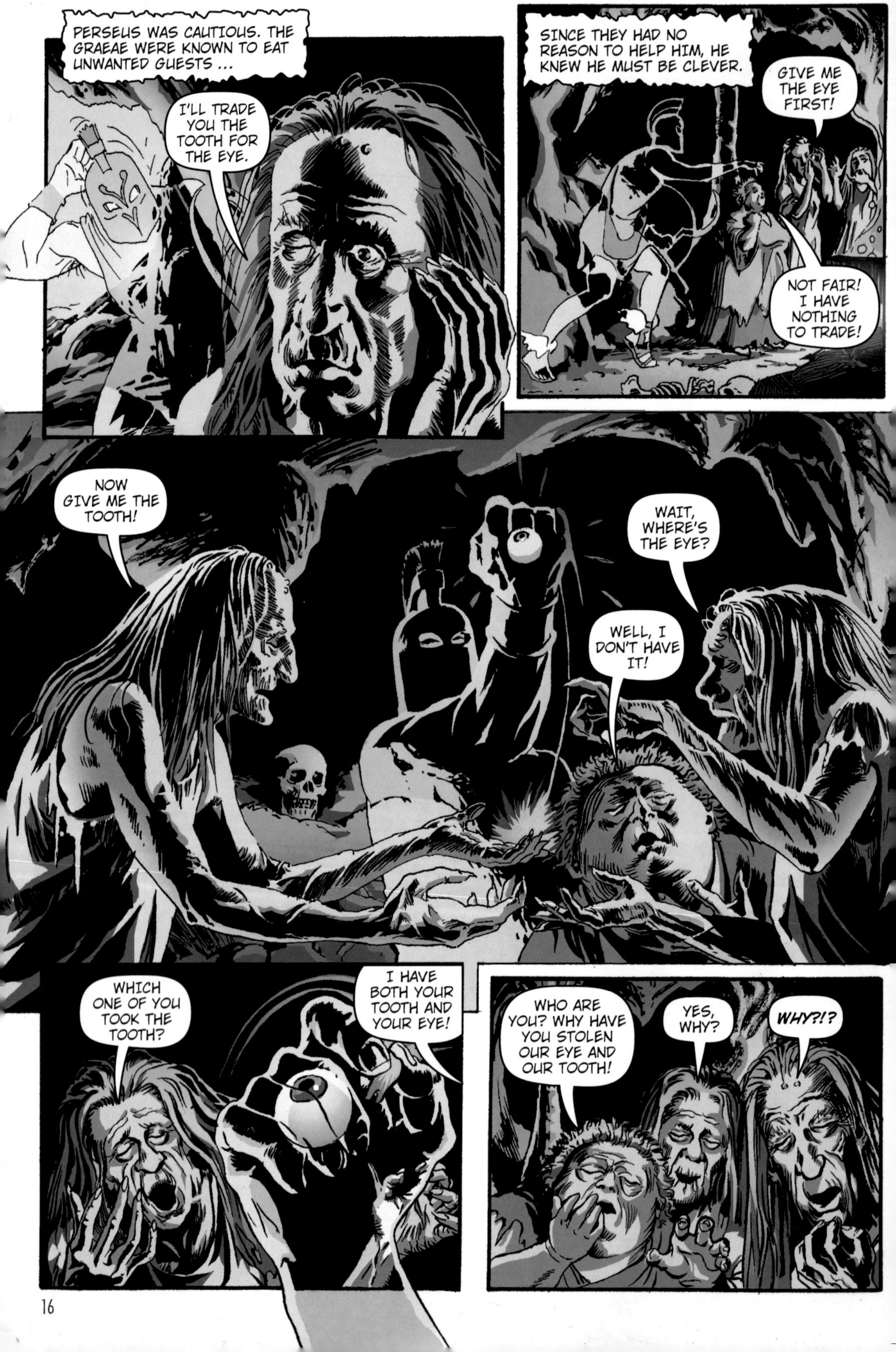
PERSEUS WAS CAUTIOUS. THE GRAEAE WERE KNOWN TO EAT UNWANTED GUESTS ...
I'LL TRADE YOU THE TOOTH FOR THE EYE.
SINCE THEY HAD NO REASON TO HELP HIM, HE KNEW HE MUST BE CLEVER.
GIVE ME THE EYE FIRST!
NOT FAIR! I HAVE NOTHING TO TRADE!
NOW GIVE ME THE TOOTH!
WAIT, WHERE'S THE EYE?
WELL, I DON'T HAVE IT!
WHICH ONE OF YOU TOOK THE TOOTH?
I HAVE BOTH YOUR TOOTH AND YOUR EYE!
WHO ARE YOU? WHY HAVE YOU STOLEN OUR EYE AND OUR TOOTH!
YES, WHY?
WHY?!?

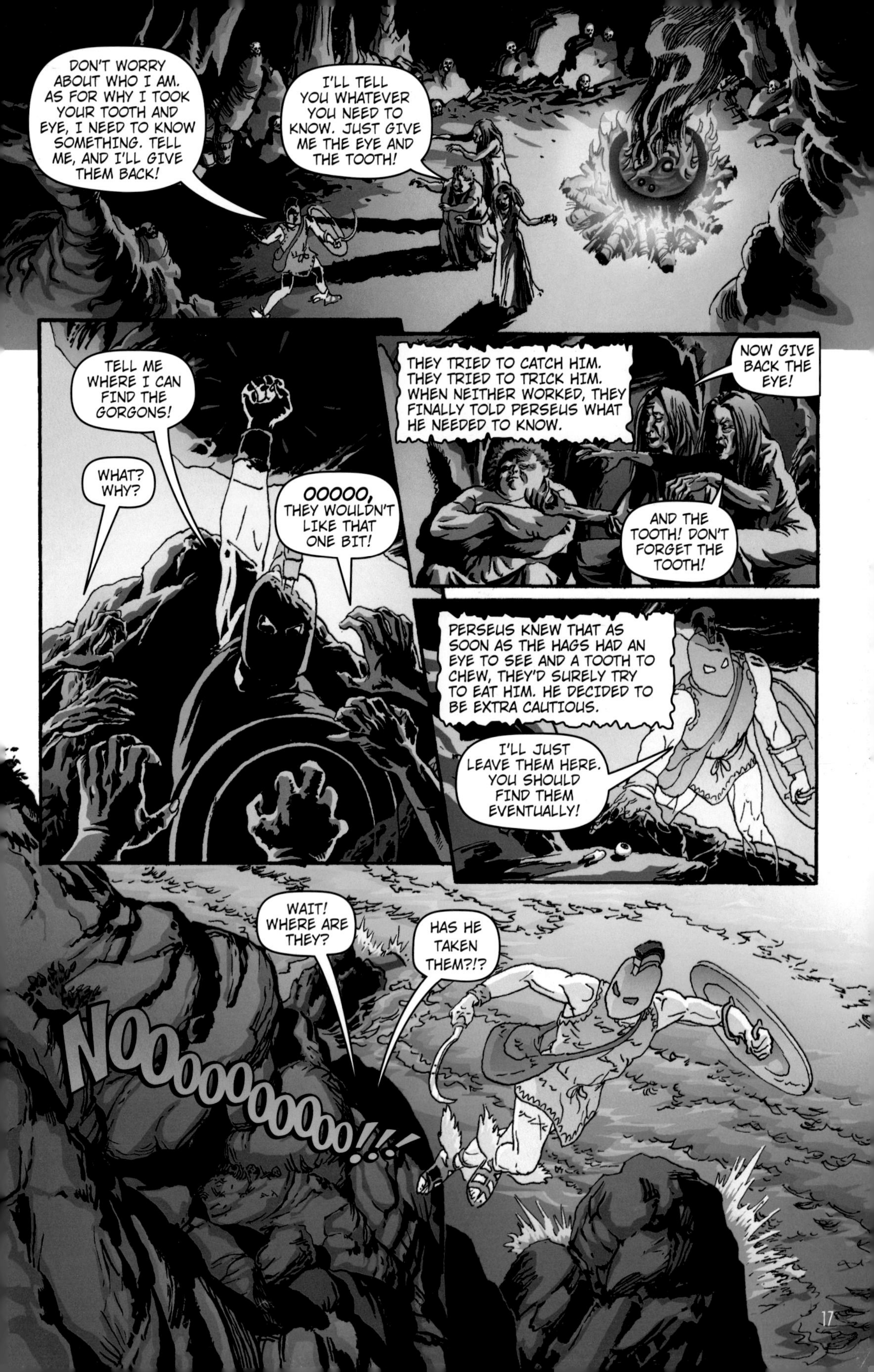
DON'T WORRY ABOUT WHO I AM. AS FOR WHY I TOOK YOUR TOOTH AND EYE, I NEED TO KNOW SOMETHING. TELL ME, AND I'LL GIVE THEM BACK!
I'LL TELL YOU WHATEVER YOU NEED TO KNOW. JUST GIVE ME THE EYE AND THE TOOTH!
TELL ME WHERE I CAN FIND THE GORGONS!
WHAT? WHY?
OOOOO, THEY WOULDN'T LIKE THAT ONE BIT!
THEY TRIED TO CATCH HIM. THEY TRIED TO TRICK HIM. WHEN NEITHER WORKED, THEY FINALLY TOLD PERSEUS WHAT HE NEEDED TO KNOW.
NOW GIVE BACK THE EYE!
AND THE TOOTH! DON'T FORGET THE TOOTH!
PERSEUS KNEW THAT AS SOON AS THE HAGS HAD AN EYE TO SEE AND A TOOTH TO CHEW, THEY'D SURELY TRY TO EAT HIM. HE DECIDED TO BE EXTRA CAUTIOUS.
I'LL JUST LEAVE THEM HERE. YOU SHOULD FIND THEM EVENTUALLY!
WAIT! WHERE ARE THEY?
HAS HE TAKEN THEM?!?
NOOOOOOOOOOO!!!!

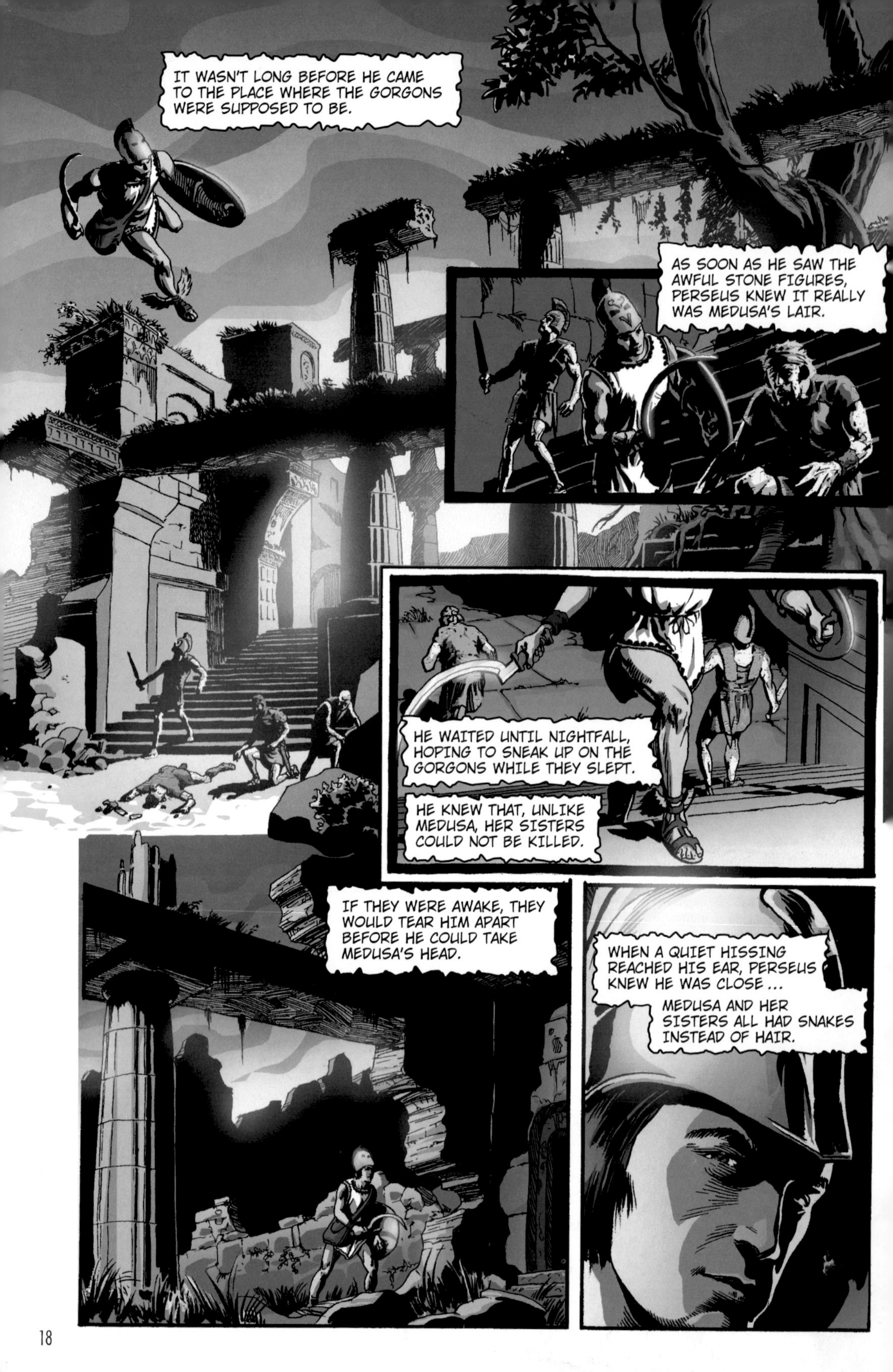
IT WASN'T LONG BEFORE HE CAME TO THE PLACE WHERE THE GORGONS WERE SUPPOSED TO BE.
AS SOON AS HE SAW THE AWFUL STONE FIGURES, PERSEUS KNEW IT REALLY WAS MEDUSA'S LAIR.
HE WAITED UNTIL NIGHTFALL, HOPING TO SNEAK UP ON THE GORGONS WHILE THEY SLEPT.
HE KNEW THAT, UNLIKE MEDUSA, HER SISTERS COULD NOT BE KILLED.
IF THEY WERE AWAKE, THEY WOULD TEAR HIM APART BEFORE HE COULD TAKE MEDUSA'S HEAD.
WHEN A QUIET HISSING REACHED HIS EAR, PERSEUS KNEW HE WAS CLOSE ...
MEDUSA AND HER SISTERS ALL HAD SNAKES INSTEAD OF HAIR.

PERSEUS WISHED HE COULD USE THE HELMET OF HADES TO APPROACH THE GORGONS.

UNFORTUNATELY, IT MADE EVERYTHING HE TOUCHED INVISIBLE TOO, INCLUDING HIS SHIELD. HE REMEMBERED ATHENA'S WARNING TO ONLY LOOK AT MEDUSA'S REFLECTION.

SINCE MEDUSA'S IMMORTAL SISTERS BOTH HAD HUGE, METALLIC WINGS, IT WASN'T HARD FOR PERSEUS TO CHOOSE THE RIGHT ONE.

SSSSSSSSSSSSSSSSSSS

VWWHHHSSSSSSST!!

PERSEUS HAD TO STRIKE SWIFTLY, BEFORE MEDUSA COULD WAKE HER SISTERS!

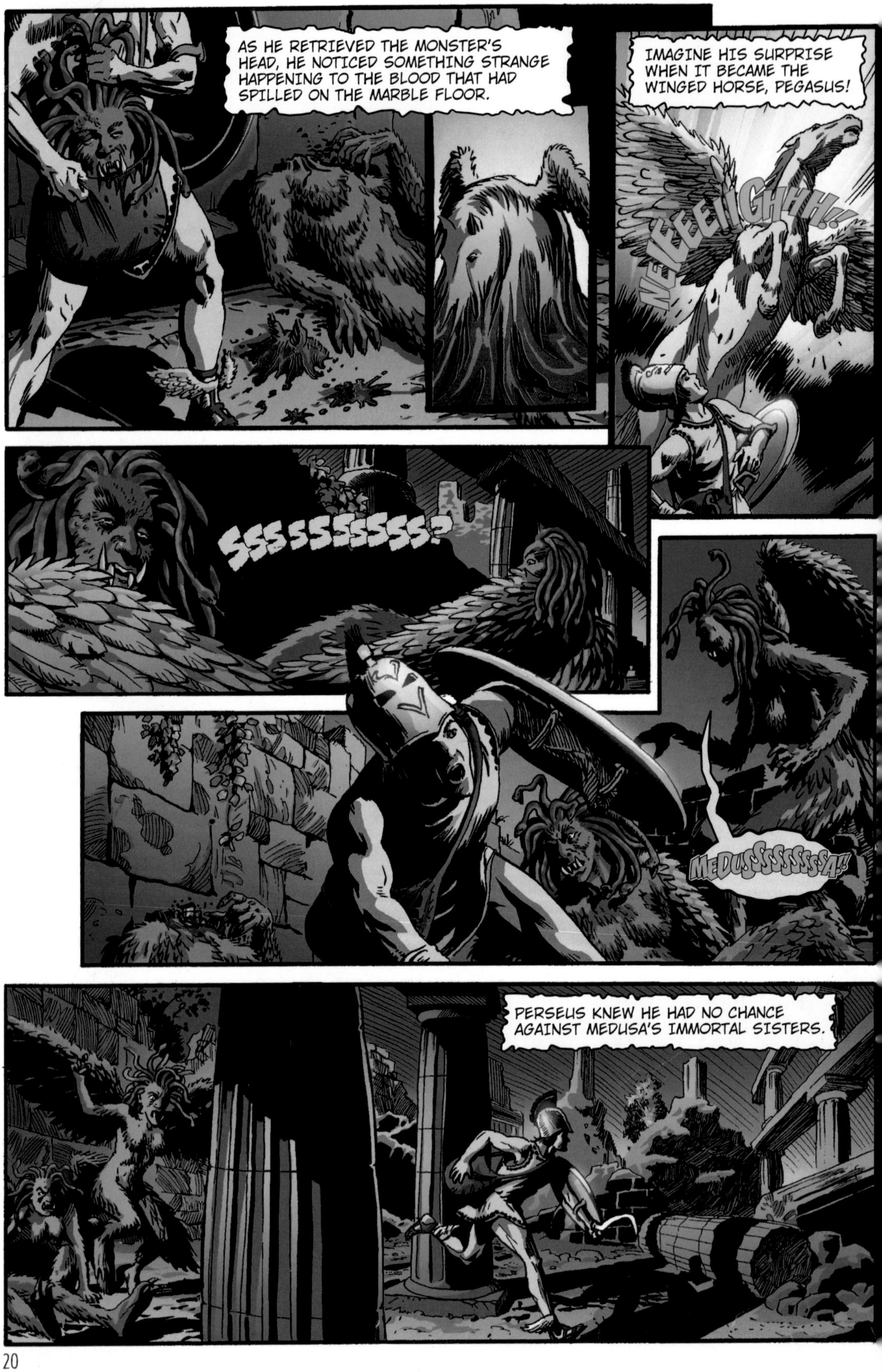

AS HE RETRIEVED THE MONSTER'S HEAD, HE NOTICED SOMETHING STRANGE HAPPENING TO THE BLOOD THAT HAD SPILLED ON THE MARBLE FLOOR.
IMAGINE HIS SURPRISE WHEN IT BECAME THE WINGED HORSE, PEGASUS!
NEIEEEIIGHHH!!
SSSSSSSSSS?
MEDUSSSSSSSSA!!
PERSEUS KNEW HE HAD NO CHANCE AGAINST MEDUSA'S IMMORTAL SISTERS.

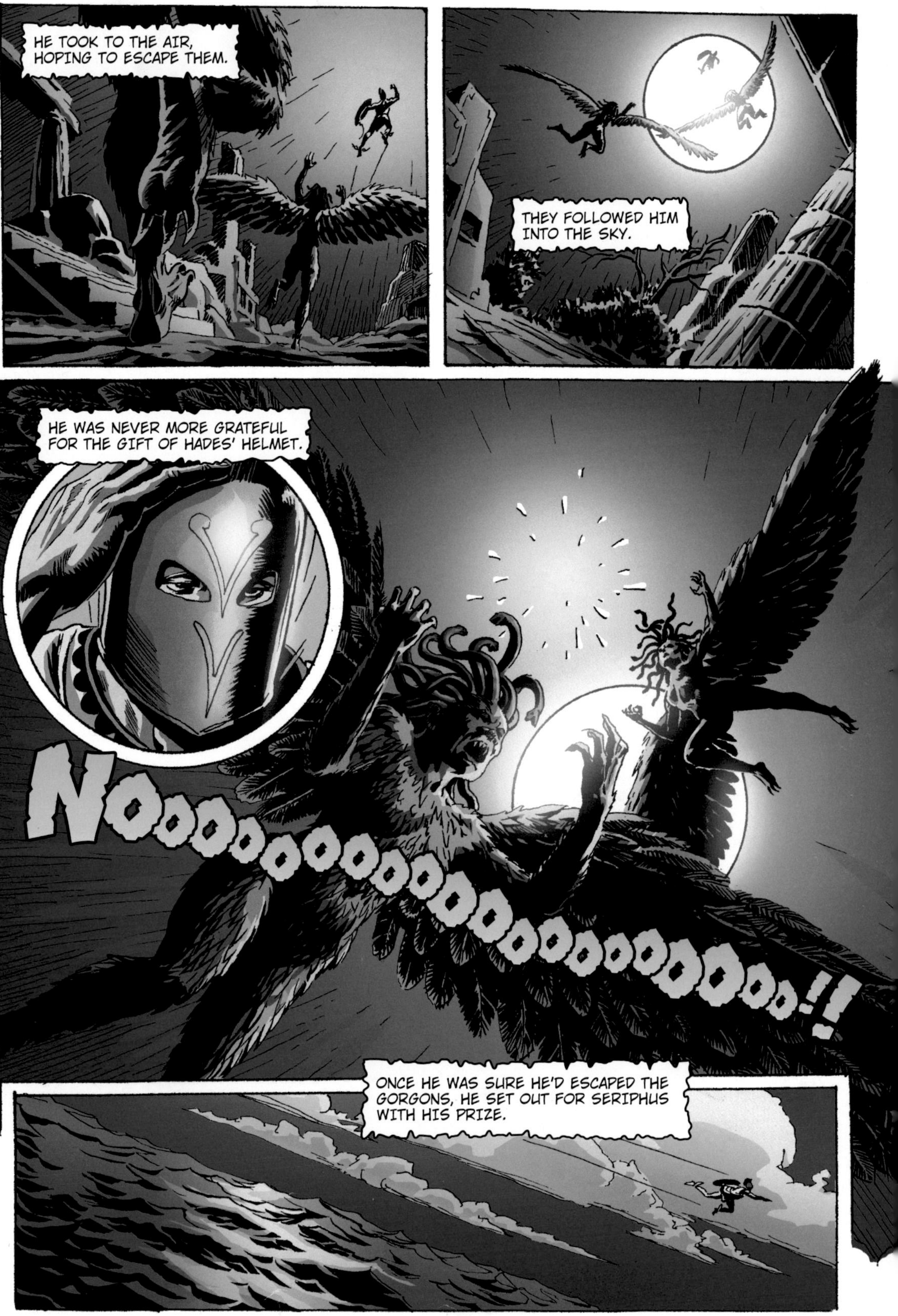
HE TOOK TO THE AIR, HOPING TO ESCAPE THEM.
THEY FOLLOWED HIM INTO THE SKY.
HE WAS NEVER MORE GRATEFUL FOR THE GIFT OF HADES' HELMET.
NOOOOOOOOOOOOOOOOOOOOOOOOO!!
ONCE HE WAS SURE HE'D ESCAPED THE GORGONS, HE SET OUT FOR SERIPHUS WITH HIS PRIZE.

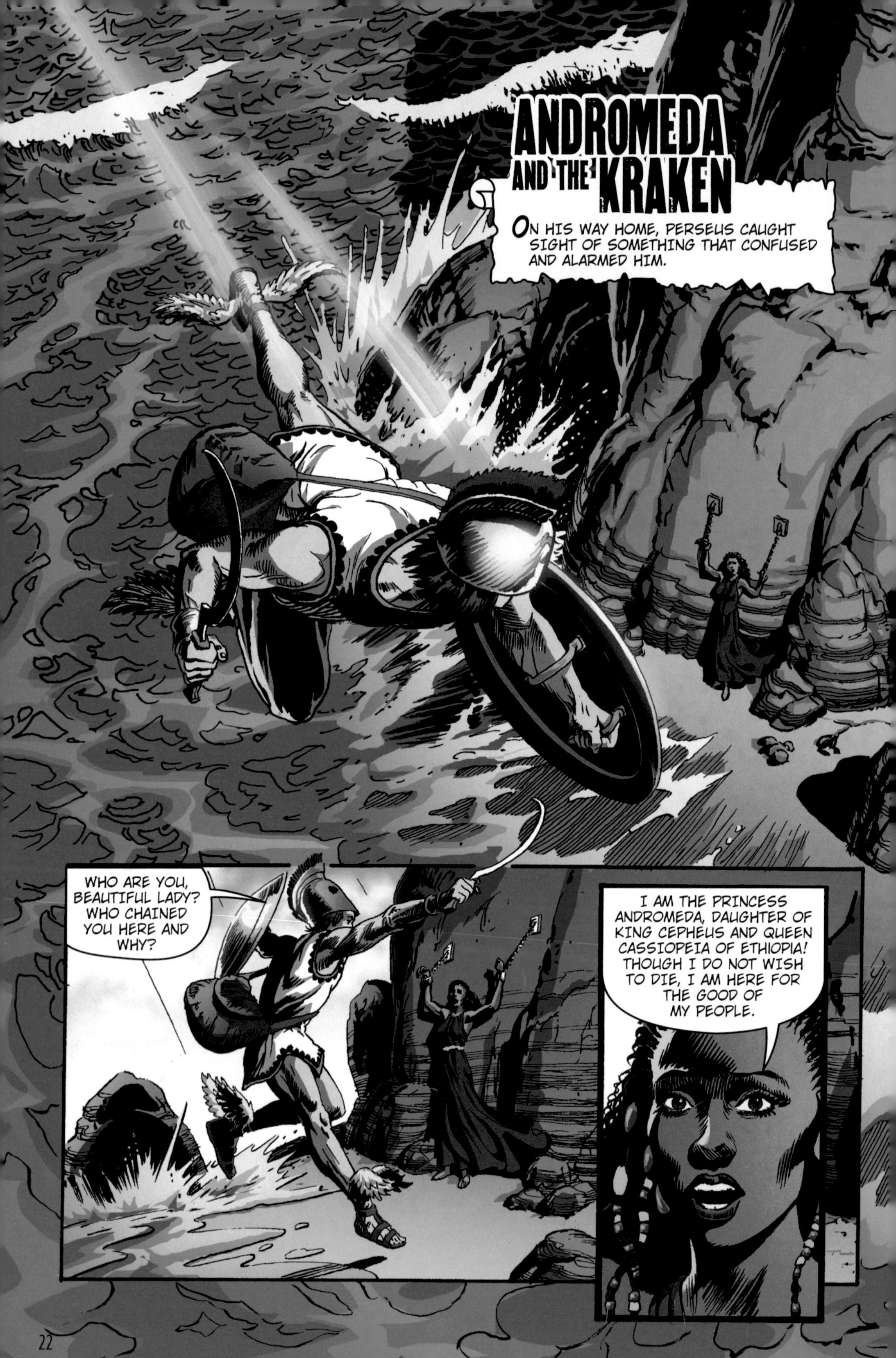

ANDROMEDA AND THE KRAKEN
ON HIS WAY HOME, PERSEUS CAUGHT SIGHT OF SOMETHING THAT CONFUSED AND ALARMED HIM.
WHO ARE YOU, BEAUTIFUL LADY? WHO CHAINED YOU HERE AND WHY?
I AM THE PRINCESS ANDROMEDA, DAUGHTER OF KING CEPHEUS AND QUEEN CASSIOPEIA OF ETHIOPIA! THOUGH I DO NOT WISH TO DIE, I AM HERE FOR THE GOOD OF MY PEOPLE.

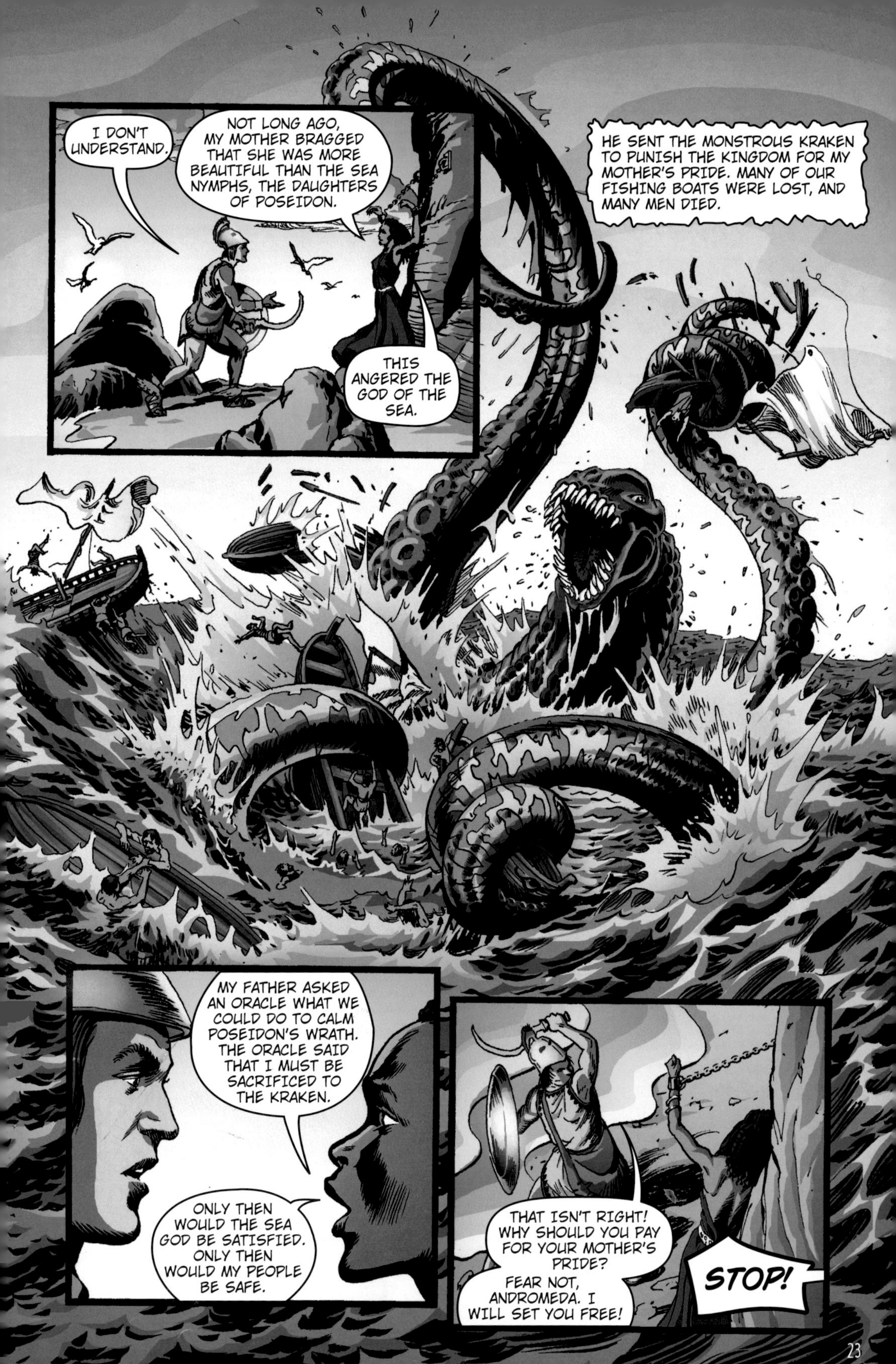
I DON'T UNDERSTAND.
NOT LONG AGO, MY MOTHER BRAGGED THAT SHE WAS MORE BEAUTIFUL THAN THE SEA NYMPHS, THE DAUGHTERS OF POSEIDON.
THIS ANGERED THE GOD OF THE SEA.
HE SENT THE MONSTROUS KRAKEN TO PUNISH THE KINGDOM FOR MY MOTHER'S PRIDE. MANY OF OUR FISHING BOATS WERE LOST, AND MANY MEN DIED.
MY FATHER ASKED AN ORACLE WHAT WE COULD DO TO CALM POSEIDON'S WRATH. THE ORACLE SAID THAT I MUST BE SACRIFICED TO THE KRAKEN.
ONLY THEN WOULD THE SEA GOD BE SATISFIED. ONLY THEN WOULD MY PEOPLE BE SAFE.
STOP!
THAT ISN'T RIGHT! WHY SHOULD YOU PAY FOR YOUR MOTHER'S PRIDE?
FEAR NOT, ANDROMEDA. I WILL SET YOU FREE!

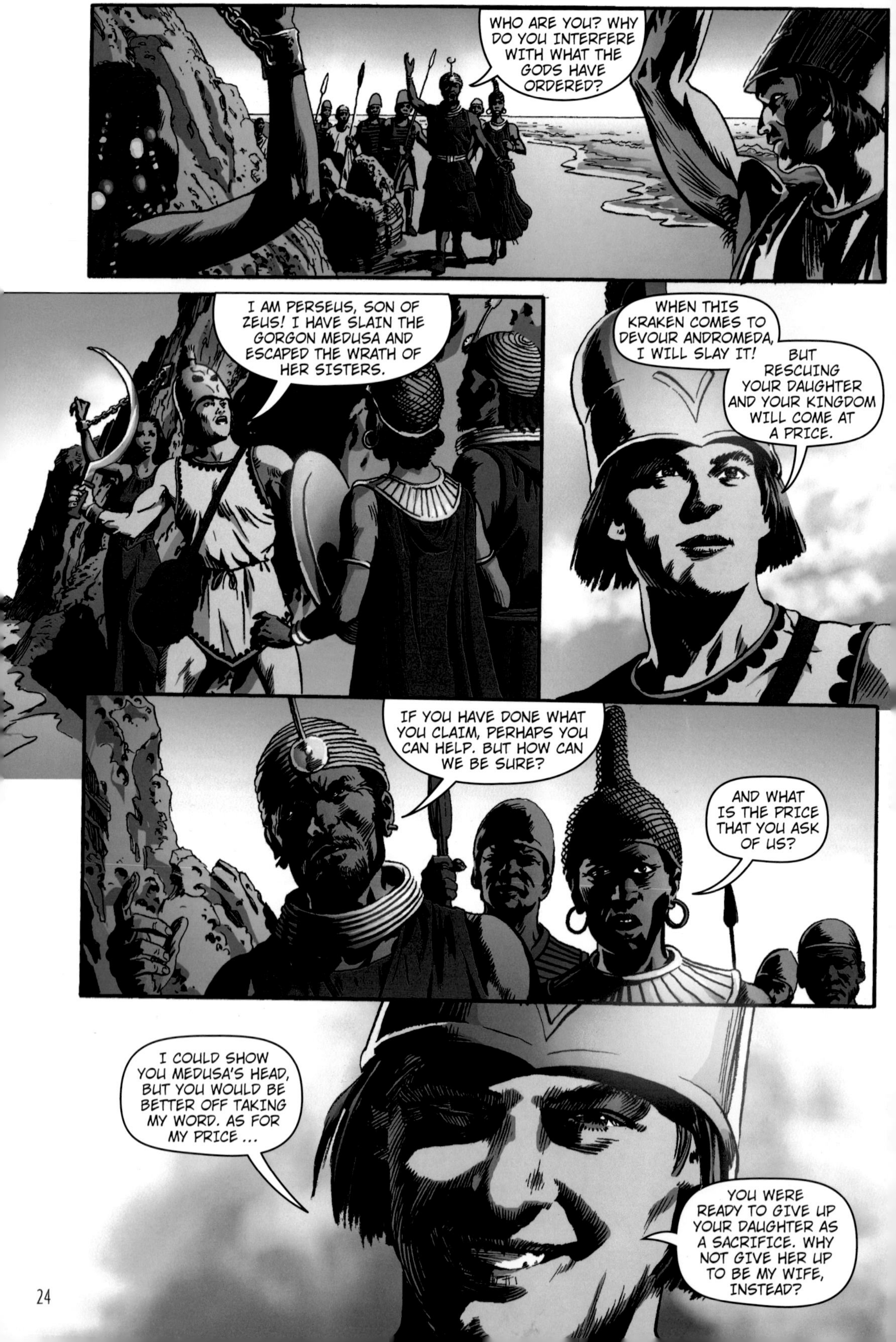
WHO ARE YOU? WHY DO YOU INTERFERE WITH WHAT THE GODS HAVE ORDERED?
I AM PERSEUS, SON OF ZEUS! I HAVE SLAIN THE GORGON MEDUSA AND ESCAPED THE WRATH OF HER SISTERS.
WHEN THIS KRAKEN COMES TO DEVOUR ANDROMEDA, I WILL SLAY IT!
BUT RESCUING YOUR DAUGHTER AND YOUR KINGDOM WILL COME AT A PRICE.
IF YOU HAVE DONE WHAT YOU CLAIM, PERHAPS YOU CAN HELP. BUT HOW CAN WE BE SURE?
AND WHAT IS THE PRICE THAT YOU ASK OF US?
I COULD SHOW YOU MEDUSA'S HEAD, BUT YOU WOULD BE BETTER OFF TAKING MY WORD. AS FOR MY PRICE ...
YOU WERE READY TO GIVE UP YOUR DAUGHTER AS A SACRIFICE. WHY NOT GIVE HER UP TO BE MY WIFE, INSTEAD?

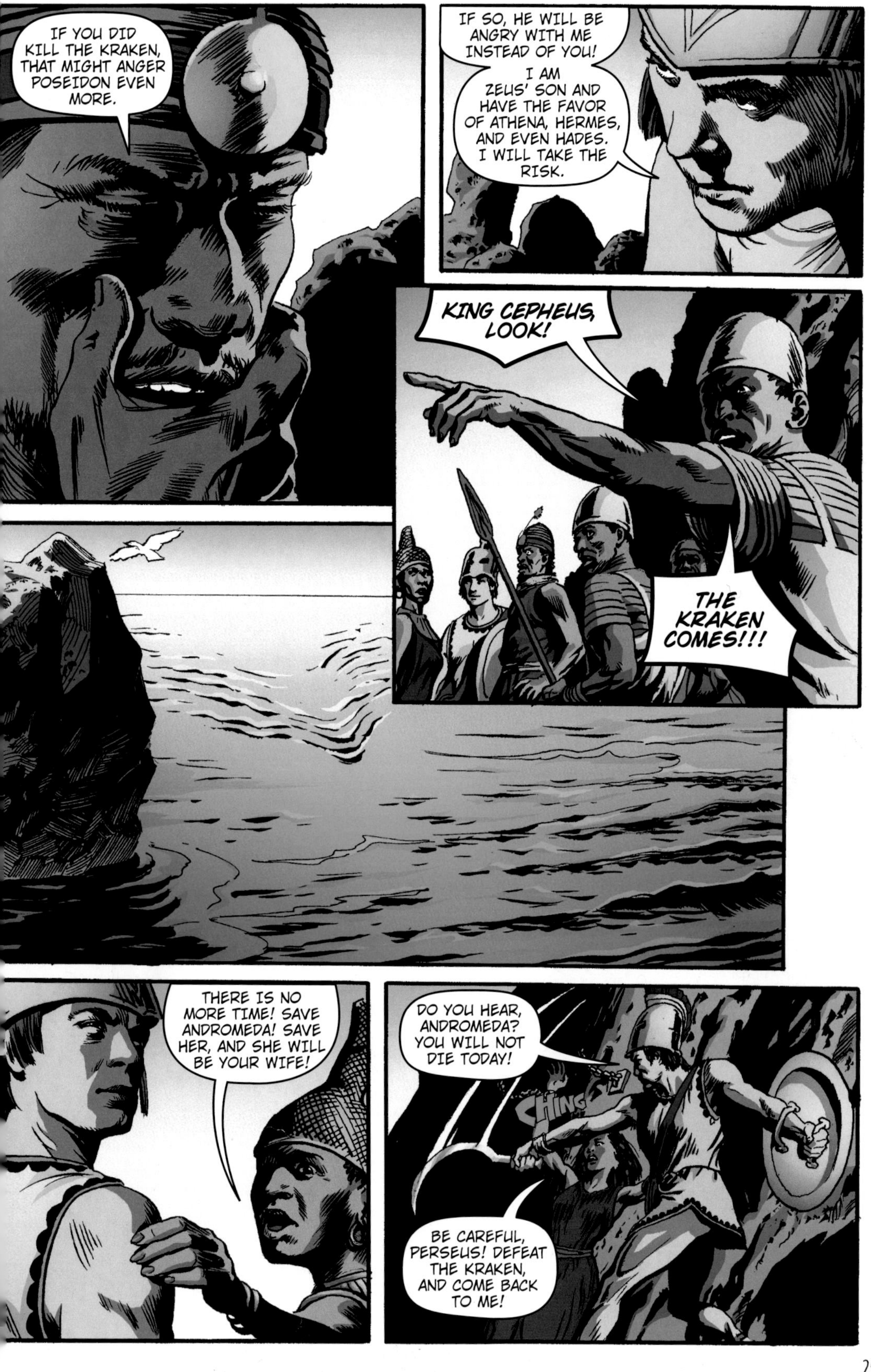

IF YOU DID KILL THE KRAKEN, THAT MIGHT ANGER POSEIDON EVEN MORE.
IF SO, HE WILL BE ANGRY WITH ME INSTEAD OF YOU!
I AM ZEUS' SON AND HAVE THE FAVOR OF ATHENA, HERMES, AND EVEN HADES. I WILL TAKE THE RISK.
KING CEPHEUS, LOOK!
THE KRAKEN COMES!!!
THERE IS NO MORE TIME! SAVE ANDROMEDA! SAVE HER, AND SHE WILL BE YOUR WIFE!
DO YOU HEAR, ANDROMEDA? YOU WILL NOT DIE TODAY!
CHING
BE CAREFUL, PERSEUS! DEFEAT THE KRAKEN, AND COME BACK TO ME!

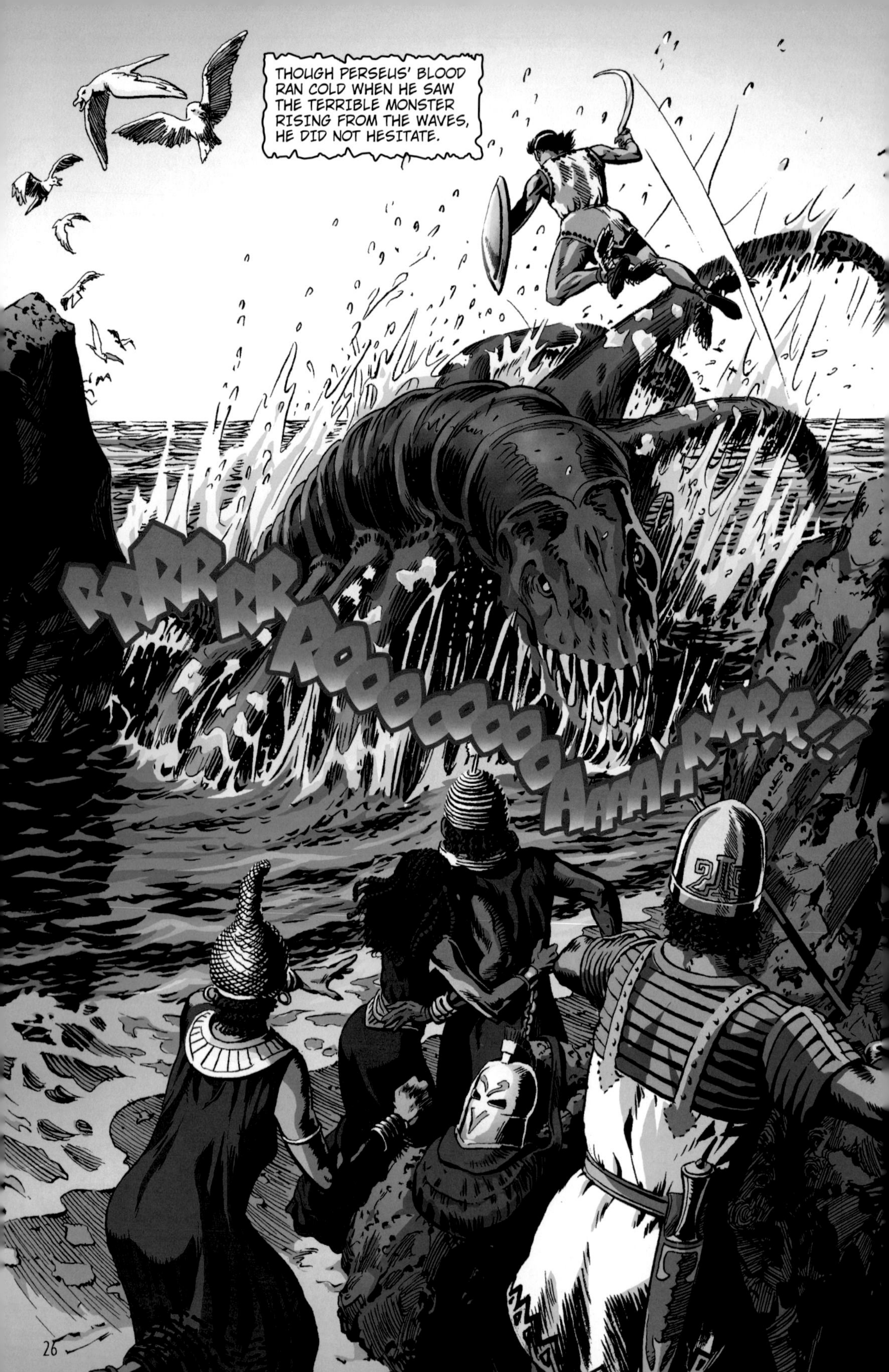
THOUGH PERSEUS' BLOOD RAN COLD WHEN HE SAW THE TERRIBLE MONSTER RISING FROM THE WAVES, HE DID NOT HESITATE.
RRRRRR ROOOOOOOO AAAAARRRR!!

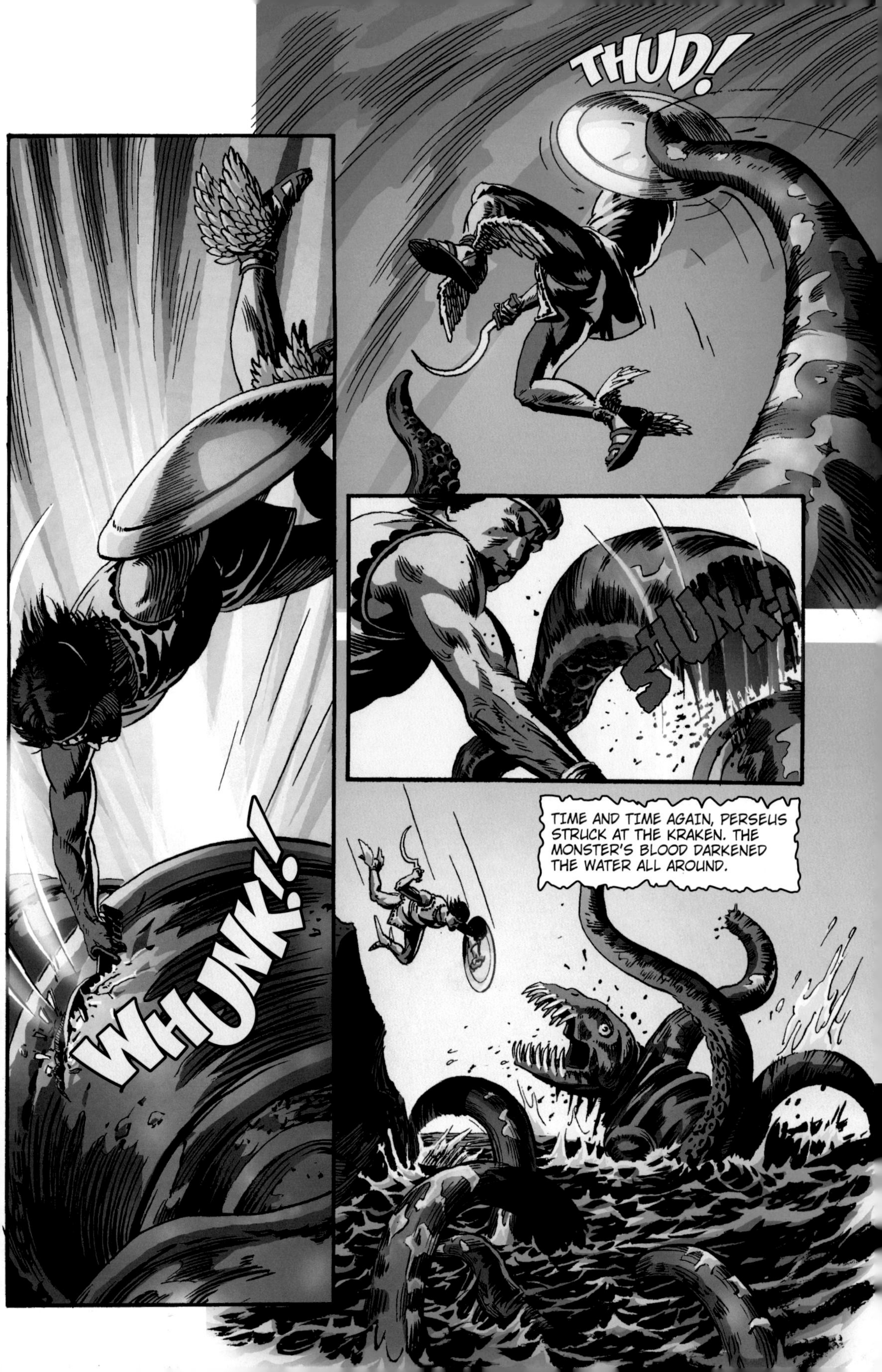
THUD!
WHUNK!!
SHUNK!!
TIME AND TIME AGAIN, PERSEUS STRUCK AT THE KRAKEN. THE MONSTER'S BLOOD DARKENED THE WATER ALL AROUND.

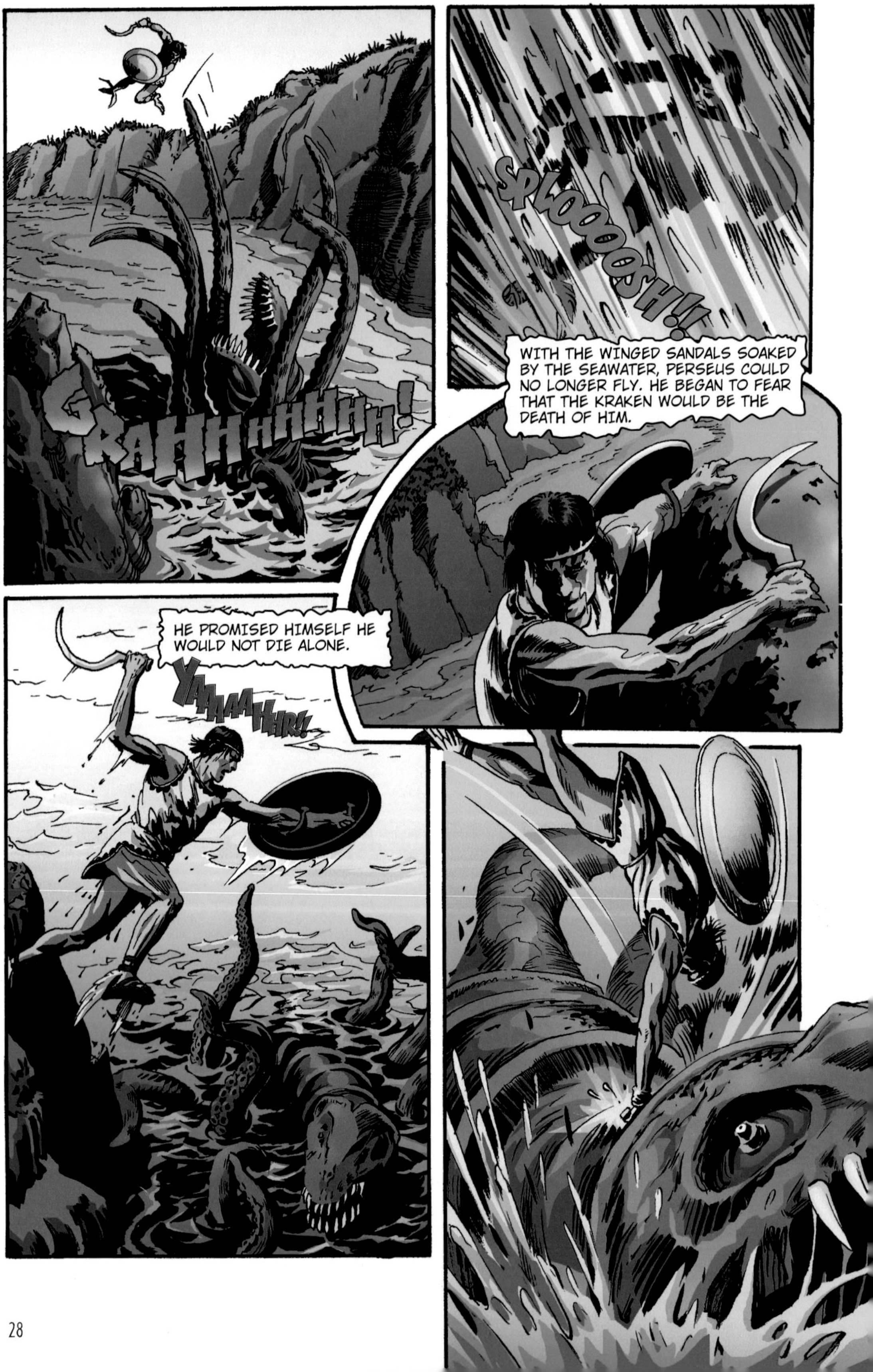
GRAHHHHHHHH!
SPLOOOOSH!!
WITH THE WINGED SANDALS SOAKED BY THE SEAWATER, PERSEUS COULD NO LONGER FLY. HE BEGAN TO FEAR THAT THE KRAKEN WOULD BE THE DEATH OF HIM.
HE PROMISED HIMSELF HE WOULD NOT DIE ALONE.
YAAAAAHHR!!

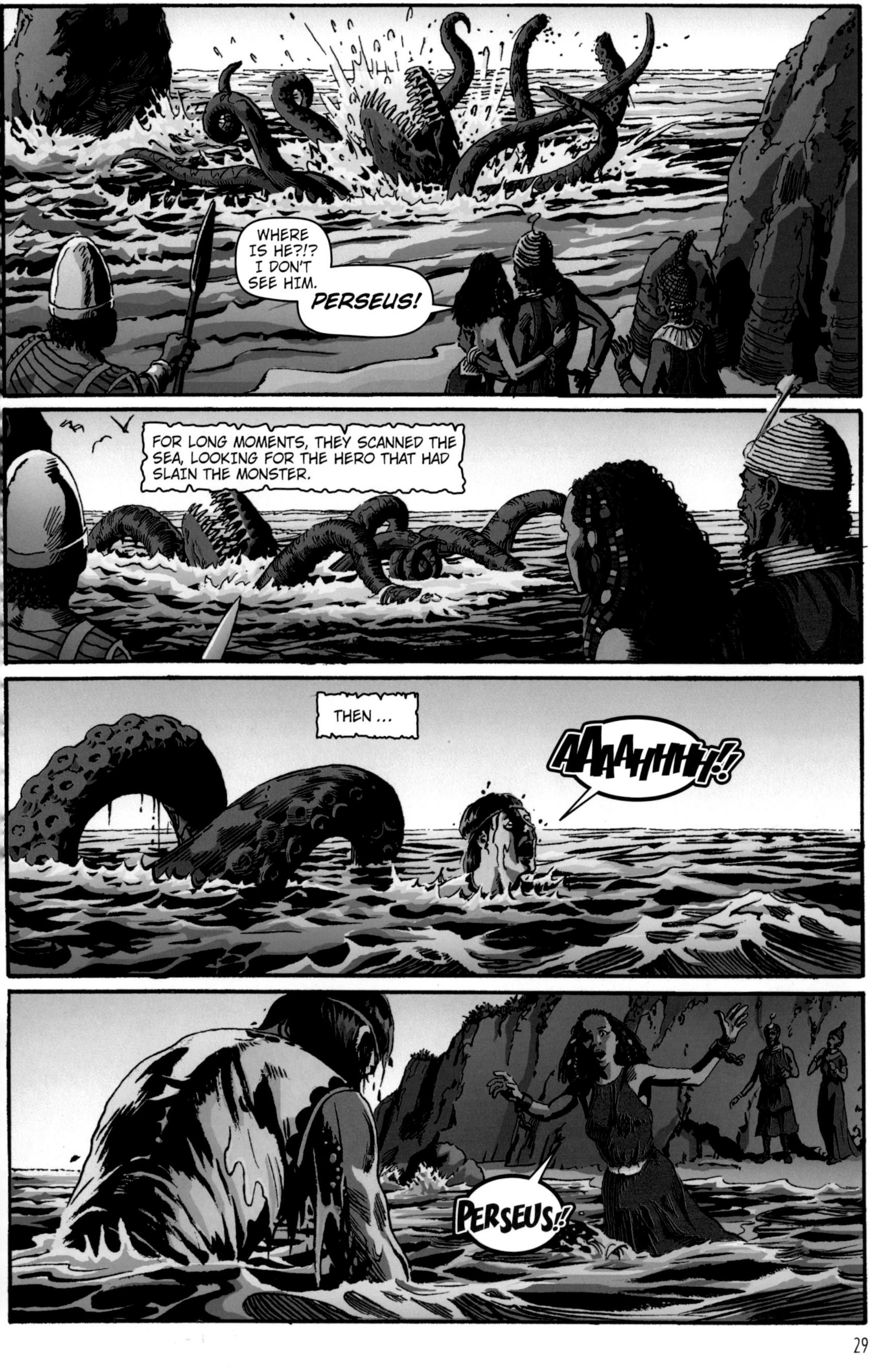
WHERE IS HE?!? I DON'T SEE HIM.
PERSEUS!
FOR LONG MOMENTS, THEY SCANNED THE SEA, LOOKING FOR THE HERO THAT HAD SLAIN THE MONSTER.
THEN ...
AAAAHHHH!!
PERSEUS!!

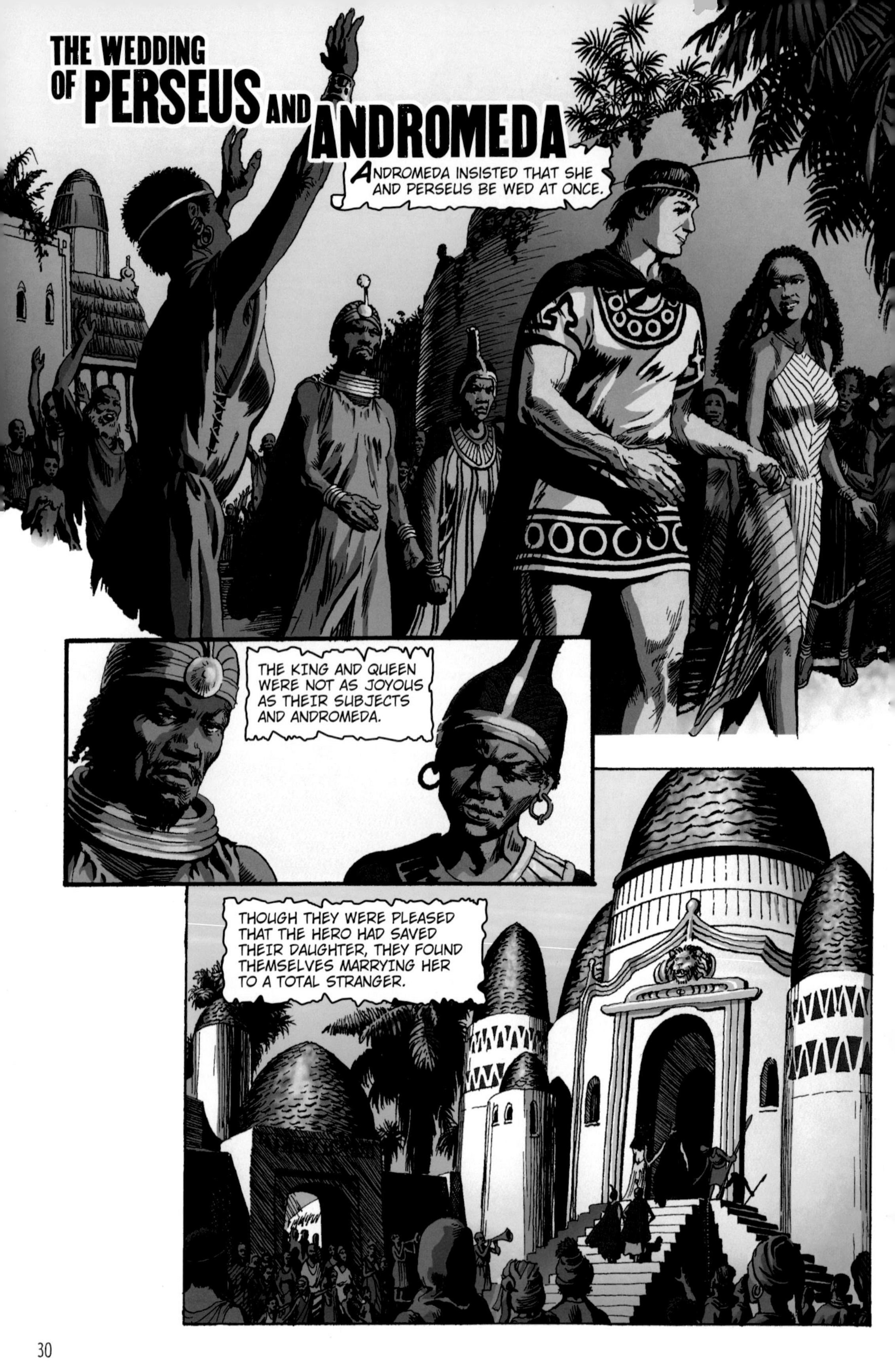
THE WEDDING OF PERSEUS AND ANDROMEDA
ANDROMEDA INSISTED THAT SHE AND PERSEUS BE WED AT ONCE.
THE KING AND QUEEN WERE NOT AS JOYOUS AS THEIR SUBJECTS AND ANDROMEDA.
THOUGH THEY WERE PLEASED THAT THE HERO HAD SAVED THEIR DAUGHTER, THEY FOUND THEMSELVES MARRYING HER TO A TOTAL STRANGER.

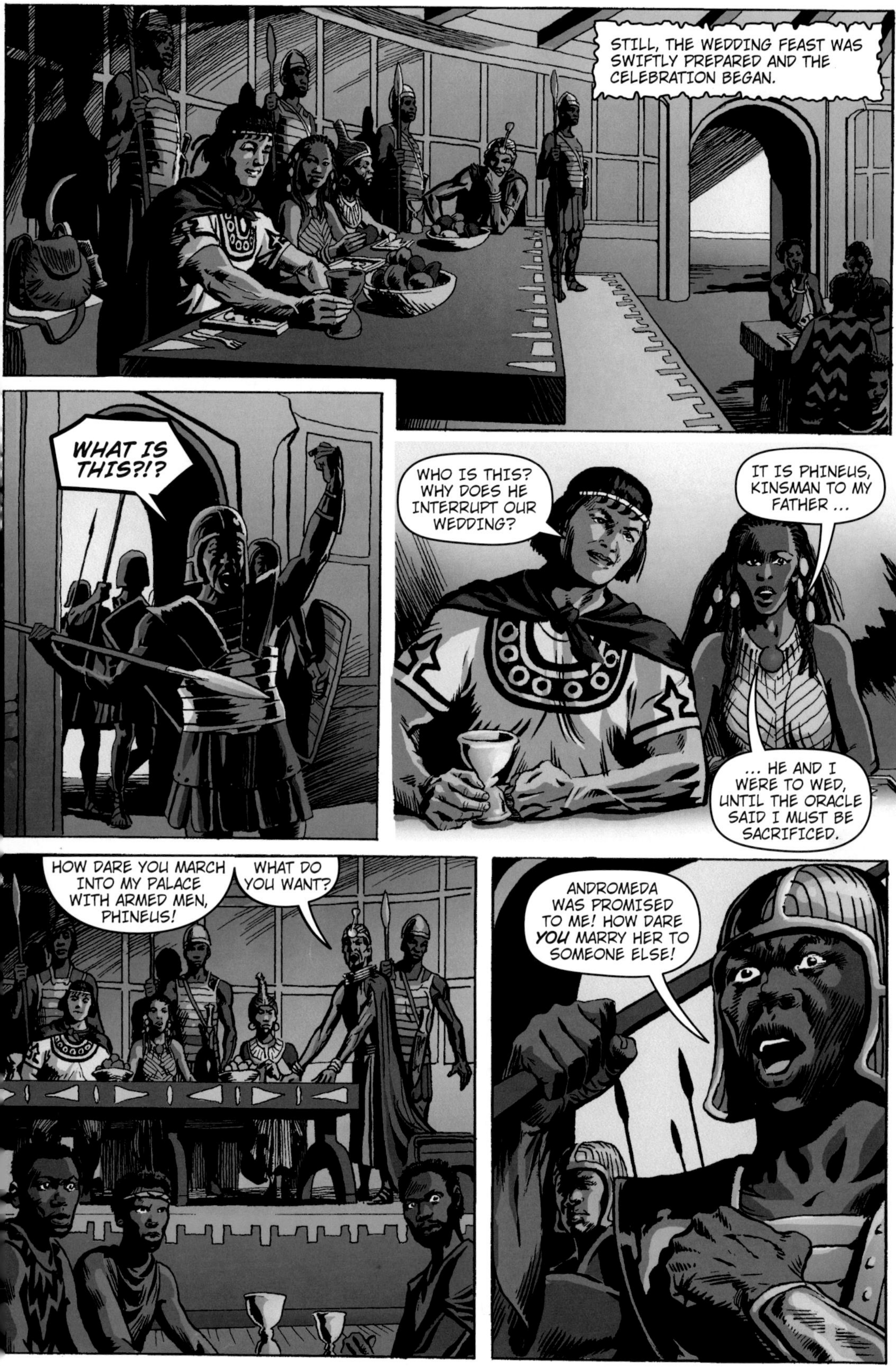
STILL, THE WEDDING FEAST WAS SWIFTLY PREPARED AND THE CELEBRATION BEGAN.
WHAT IS THIS?!?
WHO IS THIS? WHY DOES HE INTERRUPT OUR WEDDING?
IT IS PHINEUS, KINSMAN TO MY FATHER ...
... HE AND I WERE TO WED, UNTIL THE ORACLE SAID I MUST BE SACRIFICED.
HOW DARE YOU MARCH INTO MY PALACE WITH ARMED MEN, PHINEUS!
WHAT DO YOU WANT?
ANDROMEDA WAS PROMISED TO ME! HOW DARE YOU MARRY HER TO SOMEONE ELSE!

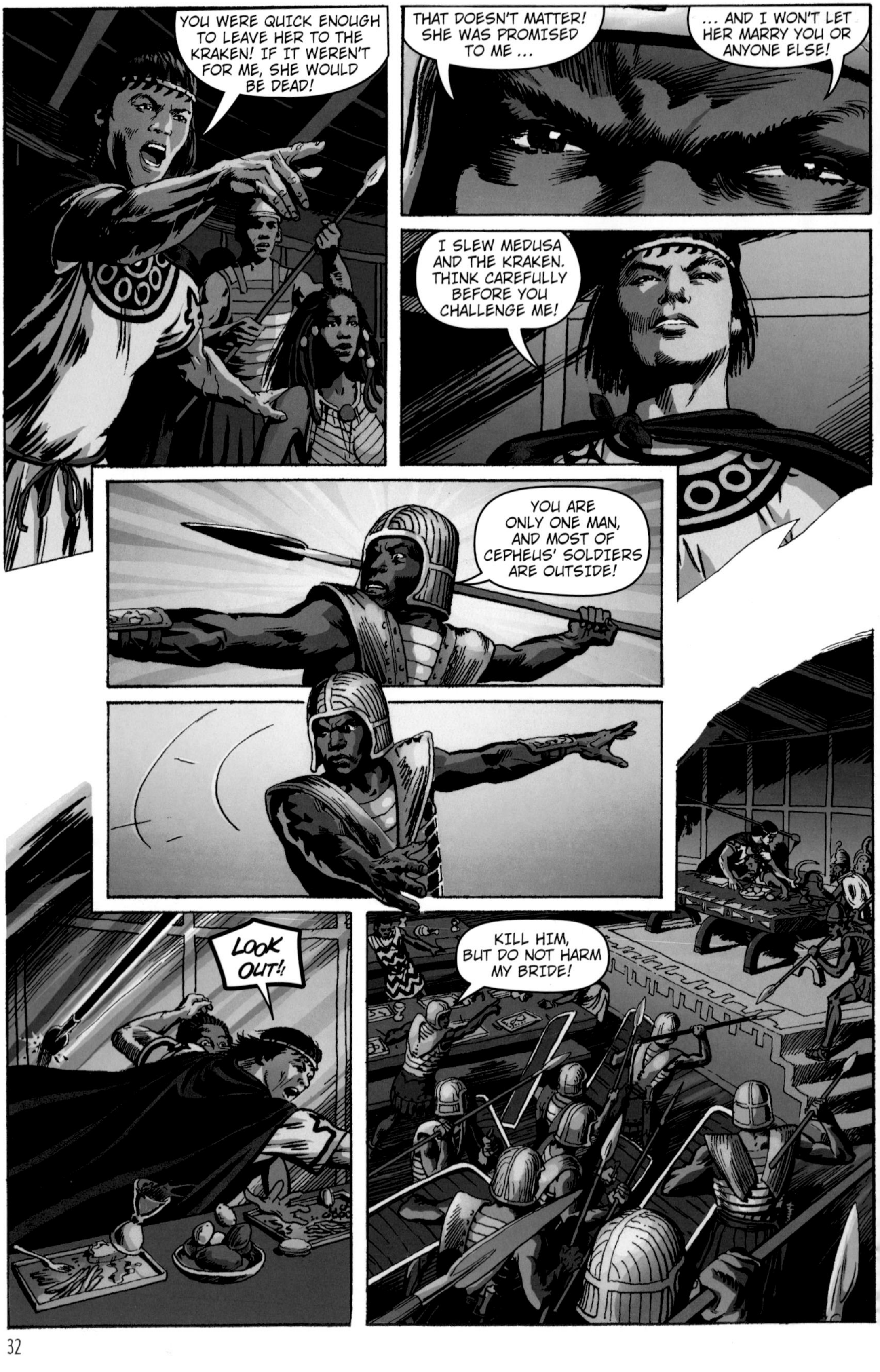
YOU WERE QUICK ENOUGH TO LEAVE HER TO THE KRAKEN! IF IT WEREN'T FOR ME, SHE WOULD BE DEAD!
THAT DOESN'T MATTER! SHE WAS PROMISED TO ME ...
... AND I WON'T LET HER MARRY YOU OR ANYONE ELSE!
I SLEW MEDUSA AND THE KRAKEN. THINK CAREFULLY BEFORE YOU CHALLENGE ME!
YOU ARE ONLY ONE MAN, AND MOST OF CEPHEUS' SOLDIERS ARE OUTSIDE!
LOOK OUT!!
KILL HIM, BUT DO NOT HARM MY BRIDE!

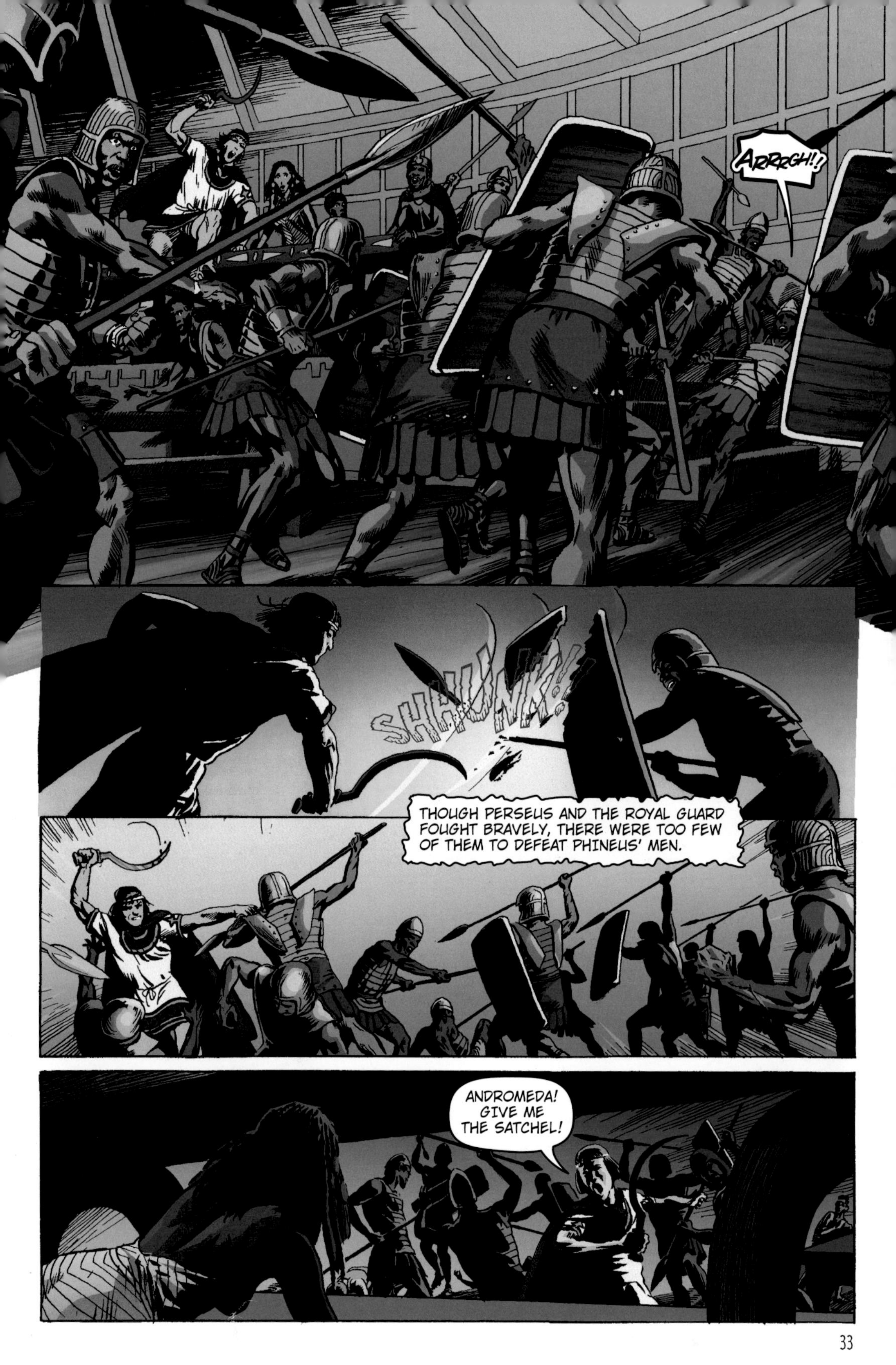
ARRRGH!!
SHHUNK!!
THOUGH PERSEUS AND THE ROYAL GUARD FOUGHT BRAVELY, THERE WERE TOO FEW OF THEM TO DEFEAT PHINEUS' MEN.
ANDROMEDA! GIVE ME THE SATCHEL!

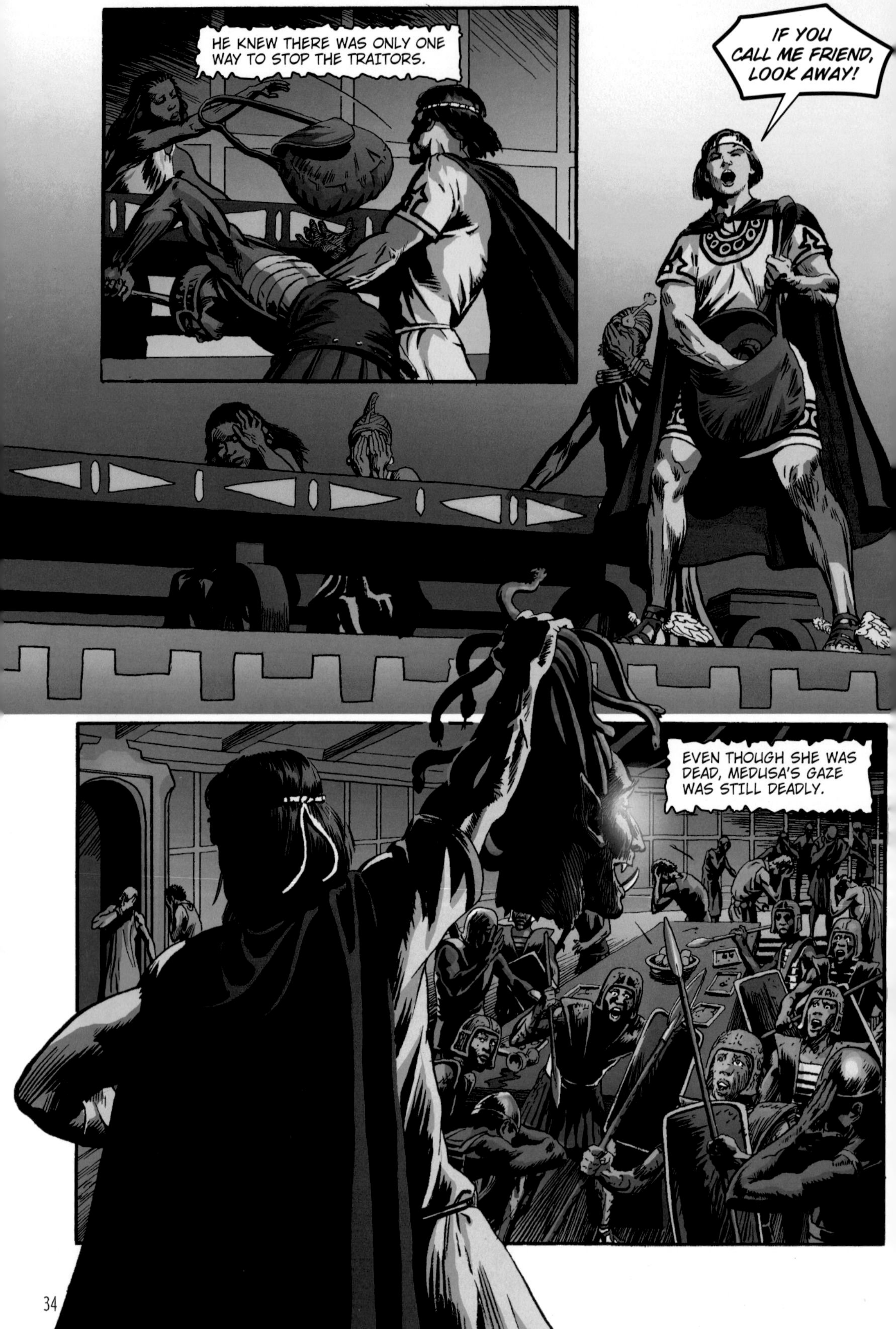

HE KNEW THERE WAS ONLY ONE WAY TO STOP THE TRAITORS.
IF YOU CALL ME FRIEND, LOOK AWAY!
EVEN THOUGH SHE WAS DEAD, MEDUSA'S GAZE WAS STILL DEADLY.

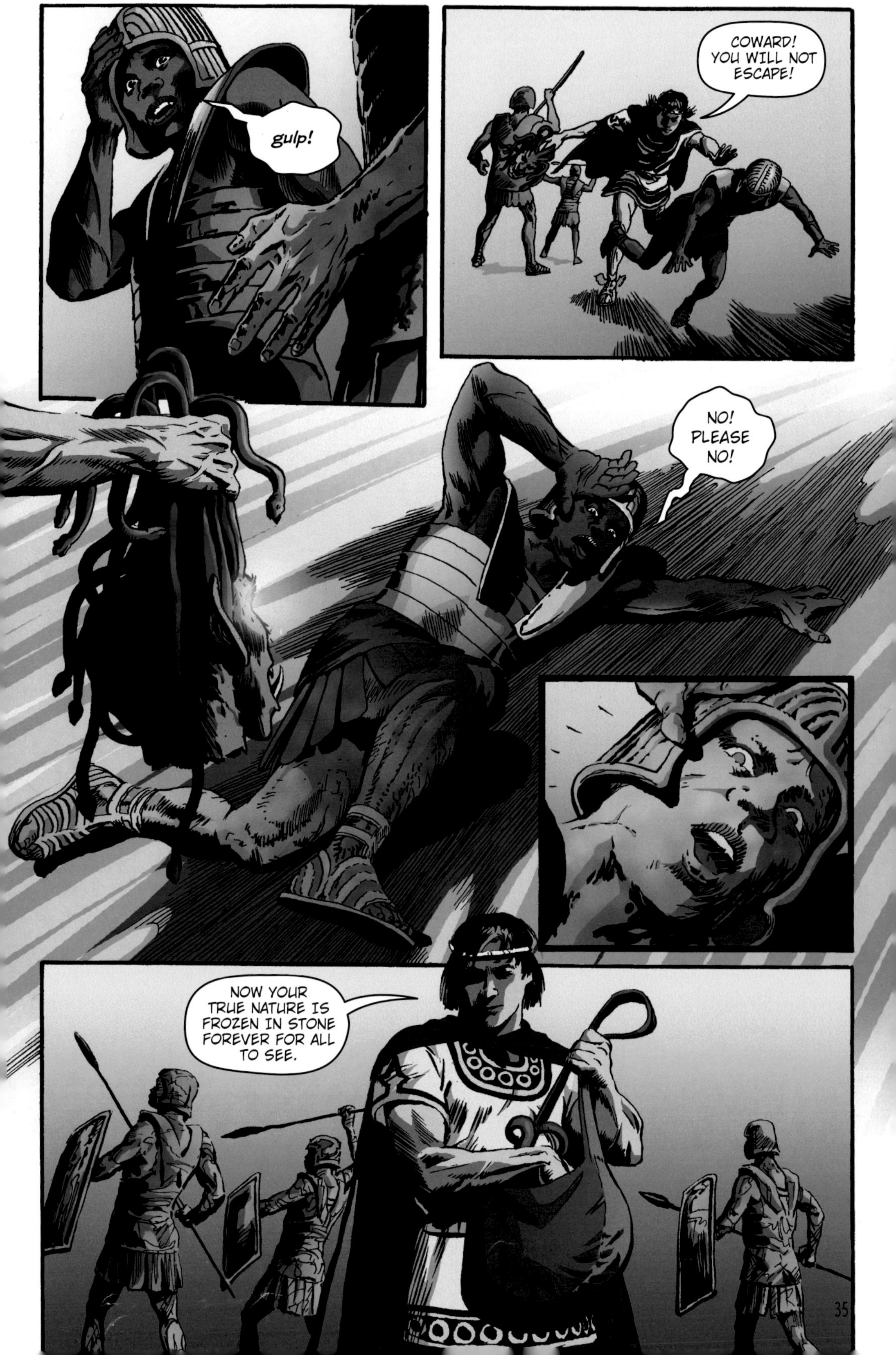
gulp!
COWARD! YOU WILL NOT ESCAPE!
NO! PLEASE NO!
NOW YOUR TRUE NATURE IS FROZEN IN STONE FOREVER FOR ALL TO SEE.

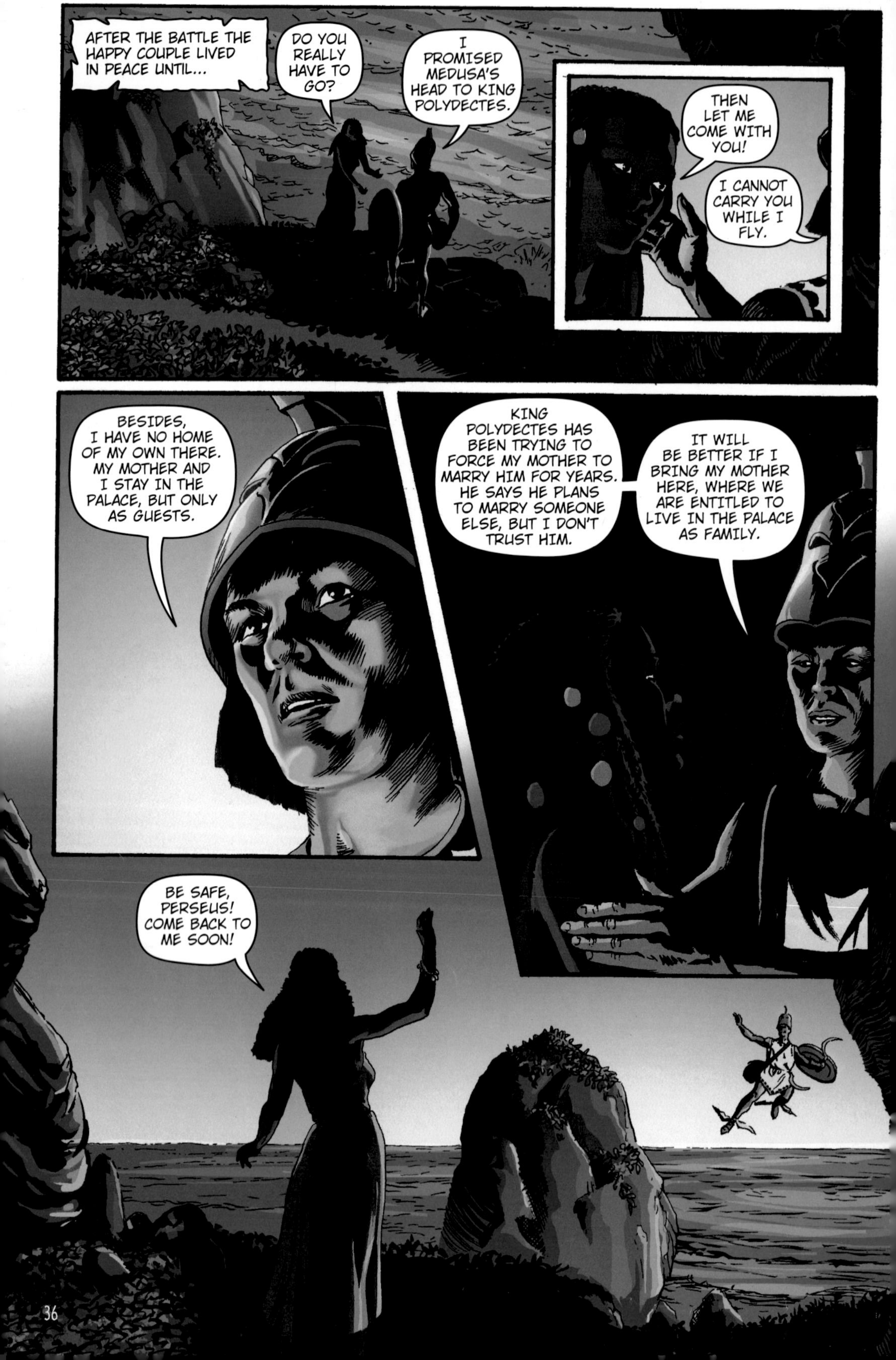
AFTER THE BATTLE THE HAPPY COUPLE LIVED IN PEACE UNTIL...
DO YOU REALLY HAVE TO GO?
I PROMISED MEDUSA'S HEAD TO KING POLYDECTES.
THEN LET ME COME WITH YOU!
I CANNOT CARRY YOU WHILE I FLY.
BESIDES, I HAVE NO HOME OF MY OWN THERE. MY MOTHER AND I STAY IN THE PALACE, BUT ONLY AS GUESTS.
KING POLYDECTES HAS BEEN TRYING TO FORCE MY MOTHER TO MARRY HIM FOR YEARS. HE SAYS HE PLANS TO MARRY SOMEONE ELSE, BUT I DON'T TRUST HIM.
IT WILL BE BETTER IF I BRING MY MOTHER HERE, WHERE WE ARE ENTITLED TO LIVE IN THE PALACE AS FAMILY.
BE SAFE, PERSEUS! COME BACK TO ME SOON!

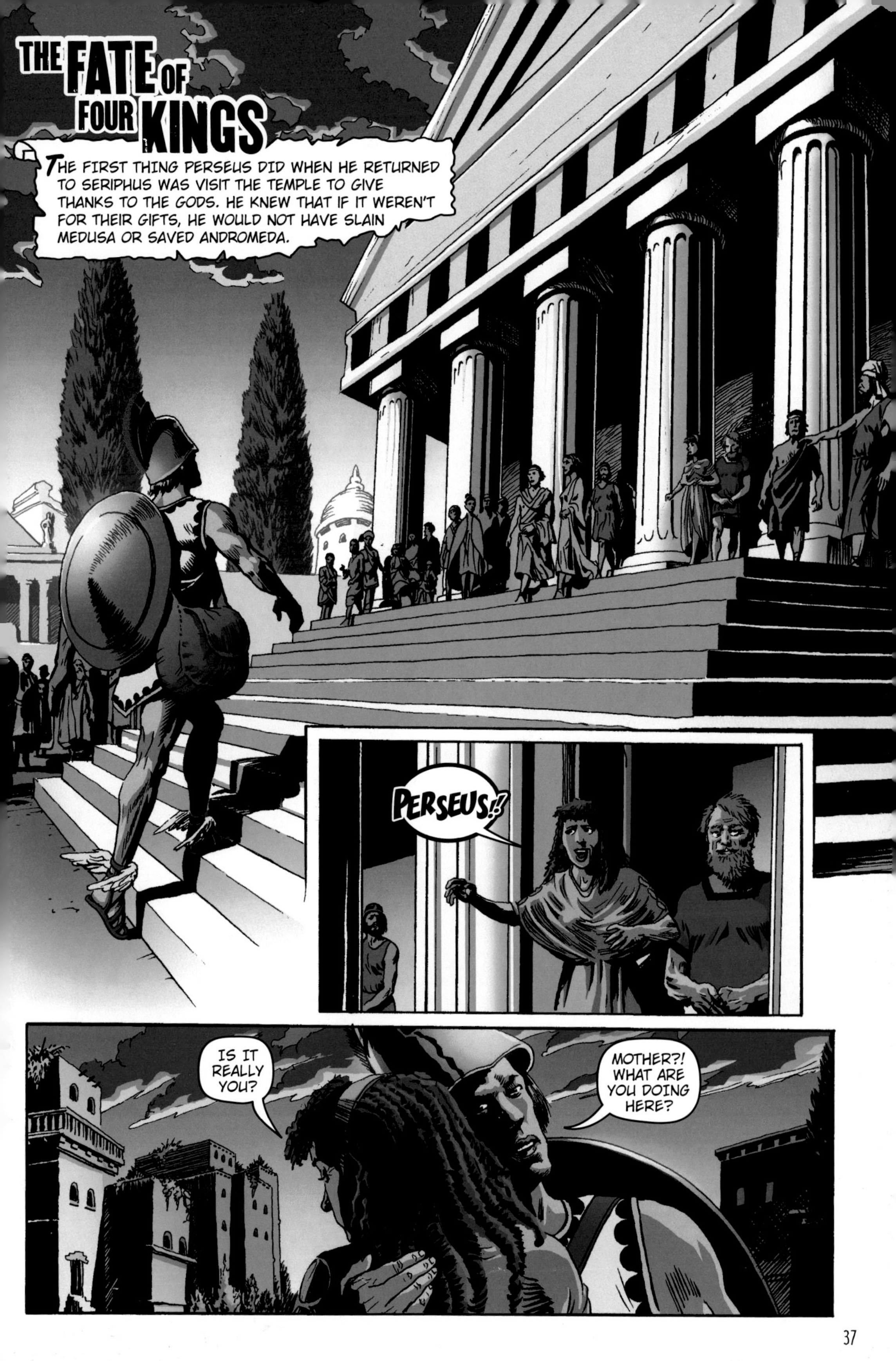
THE FATE OF FOUR KINGS
THE FIRST THING PERSEUS DID WHEN HE RETURNED TO SERIPHUS WAS VISIT THE TEMPLE TO GIVE THANKS TO THE GODS. HE KNEW THAT IF IT WEREN'T FOR THEIR GIFTS, HE WOULD NOT HAVE SLAIN MEDUSA OR SAVED ANDROMEDA.
PERSEUS!?
IS IT REALLY YOU?
MOTHER?! WHAT ARE YOU DOING HERE?

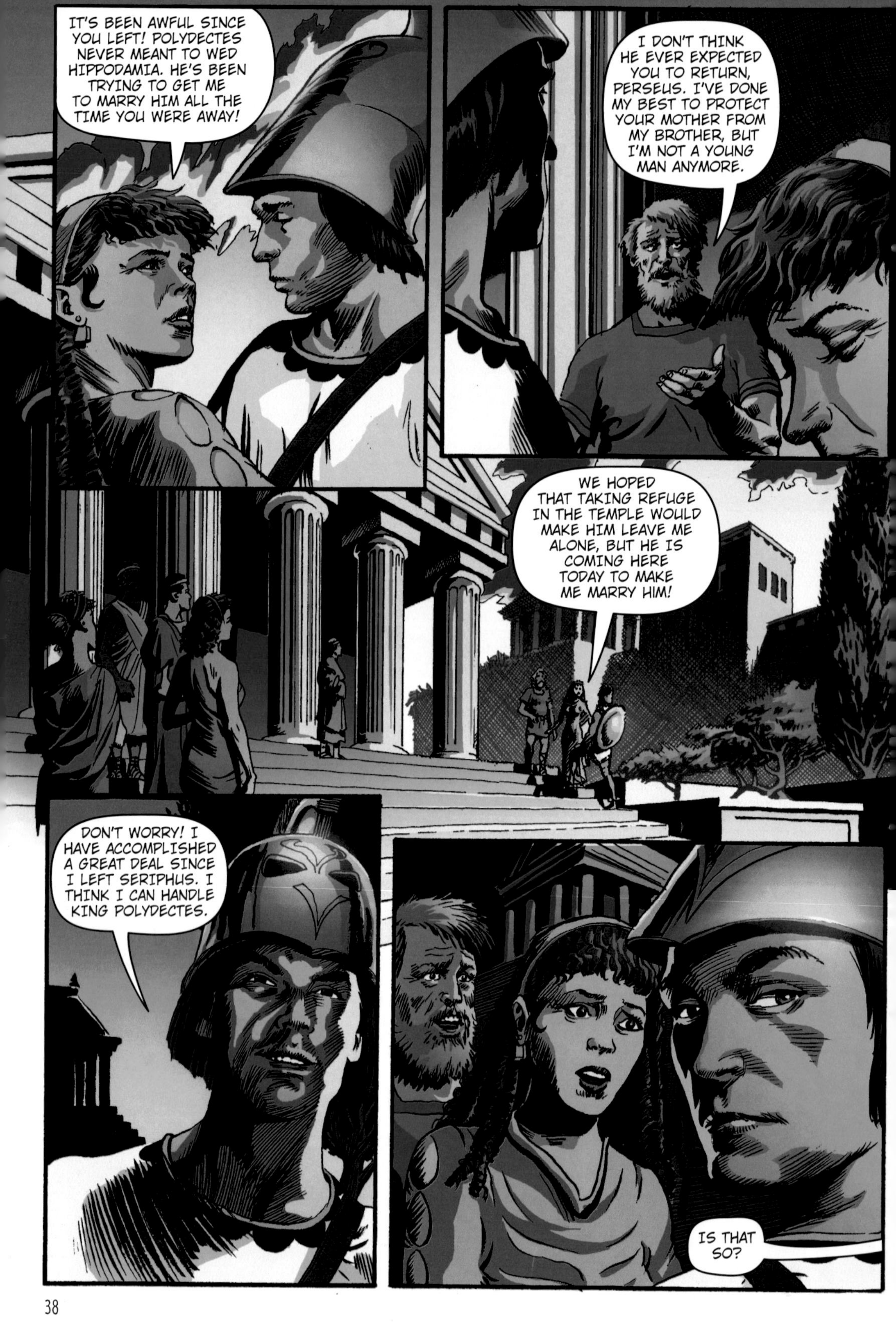
IT'S BEEN AWFUL SINCE YOU LEFT! POLYDECTES NEVER MEANT TO WED HIPPODAMIA. HE'S BEEN TRYING TO GET ME TO MARRY HIM ALL THE TIME YOU WERE AWAY!
I DON'T THINK HE EVER EXPECTED YOU TO RETURN, PERSEUS. I'VE DONE MY BEST TO PROTECT YOUR MOTHER FROM MY BROTHER, BUT I'M NOT A YOUNG MAN ANYMORE.
WE HOPED THAT TAKING REFUGE IN THE TEMPLE WOULD MAKE HIM LEAVE ME ALONE, BUT HE IS COMING HERE TODAY TO MAKE ME MARRY HIM!
DON'T WORRY! I HAVE ACCOMPLISHED A GREAT DEAL SINCE I LEFT SERIPHUS. I THINK I CAN HANDLE KING POLYDECTES.
IS THAT SO?

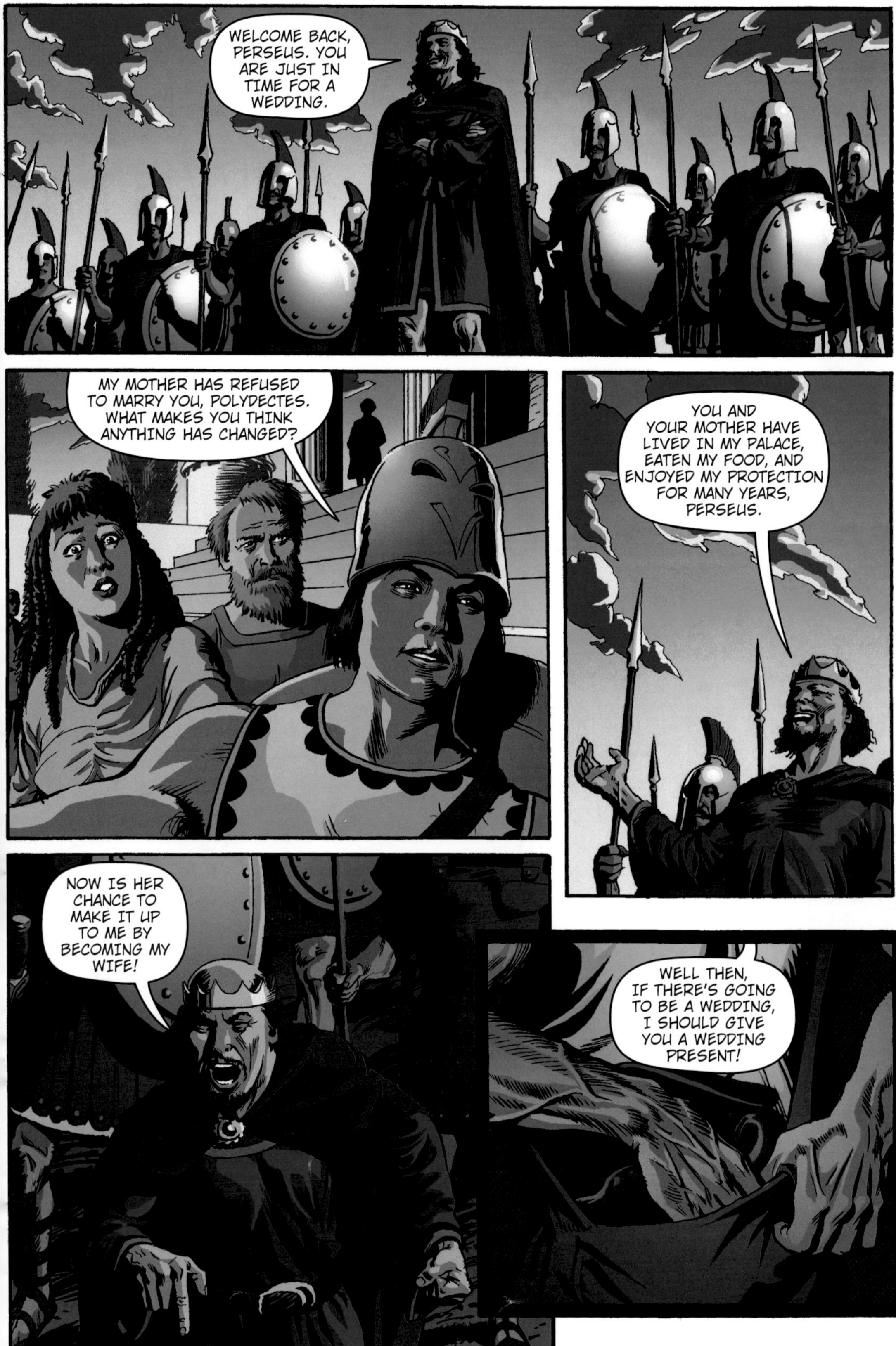
WELCOME BACK, PERSEUS. YOU ARE JUST IN TIME FOR A WEDDING.
MY MOTHER HAS REFUSED TO MARRY YOU, POLYDECTES. WHAT MAKES YOU THINK ANYTHING HAS CHANGED?
YOU AND YOUR MOTHER HAVE LIVED IN MY PALACE, EATEN MY FOOD, AND ENJOYED MY PROTECTION FOR MANY YEARS, PERSEUS.
NOW IS HER CHANCE TO MAKE IT UP TO ME BY BECOMING MY WIFE!
WELL THEN, IF THERE'S GOING TO BE A WEDDING, I SHOULD GIVE YOU A WEDDING PRESENT!

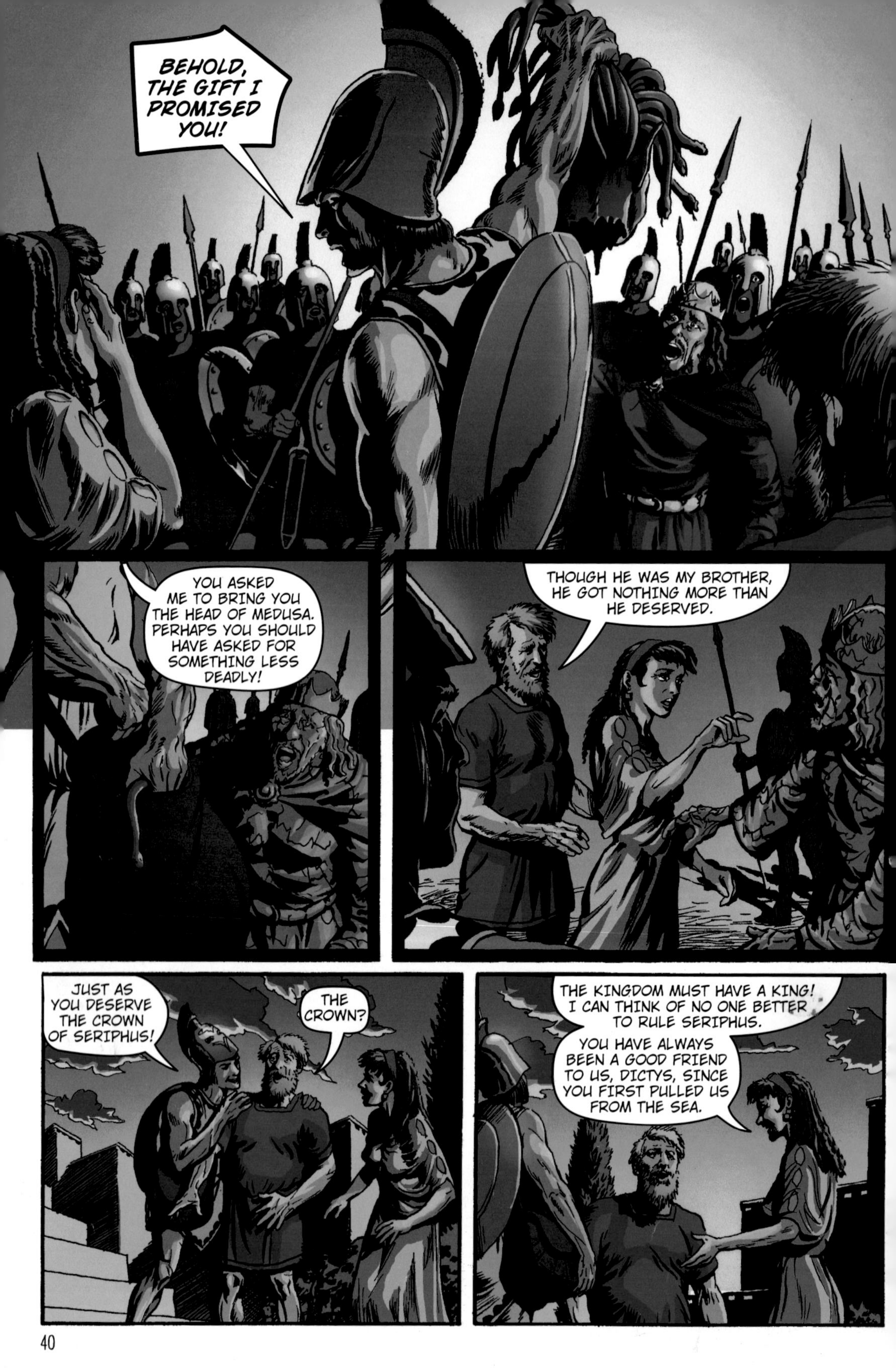
BEHOLD, THE GIFT I PROMISED YOU!
YOU ASKED ME TO BRING YOU THE HEAD OF MEDUSA. PERHAPS YOU SHOULD HAVE ASKED FOR SOMETHING LESS DEADLY!
THOUGH HE WAS MY BROTHER, HE GOT NOTHING MORE THAN HE DESERVED.
JUST AS YOU DESERVE THE CROWN OF SERIPHUS!
THE CROWN?
THE KINGDOM MUST HAVE A KING! I CAN THINK OF NO ONE BETTER TO RULE SERIPHUS.
YOU HAVE ALWAYS BEEN A GOOD FRIEND TO US, DICTYS, SINCE YOU FIRST PULLED US FROM THE SEA.

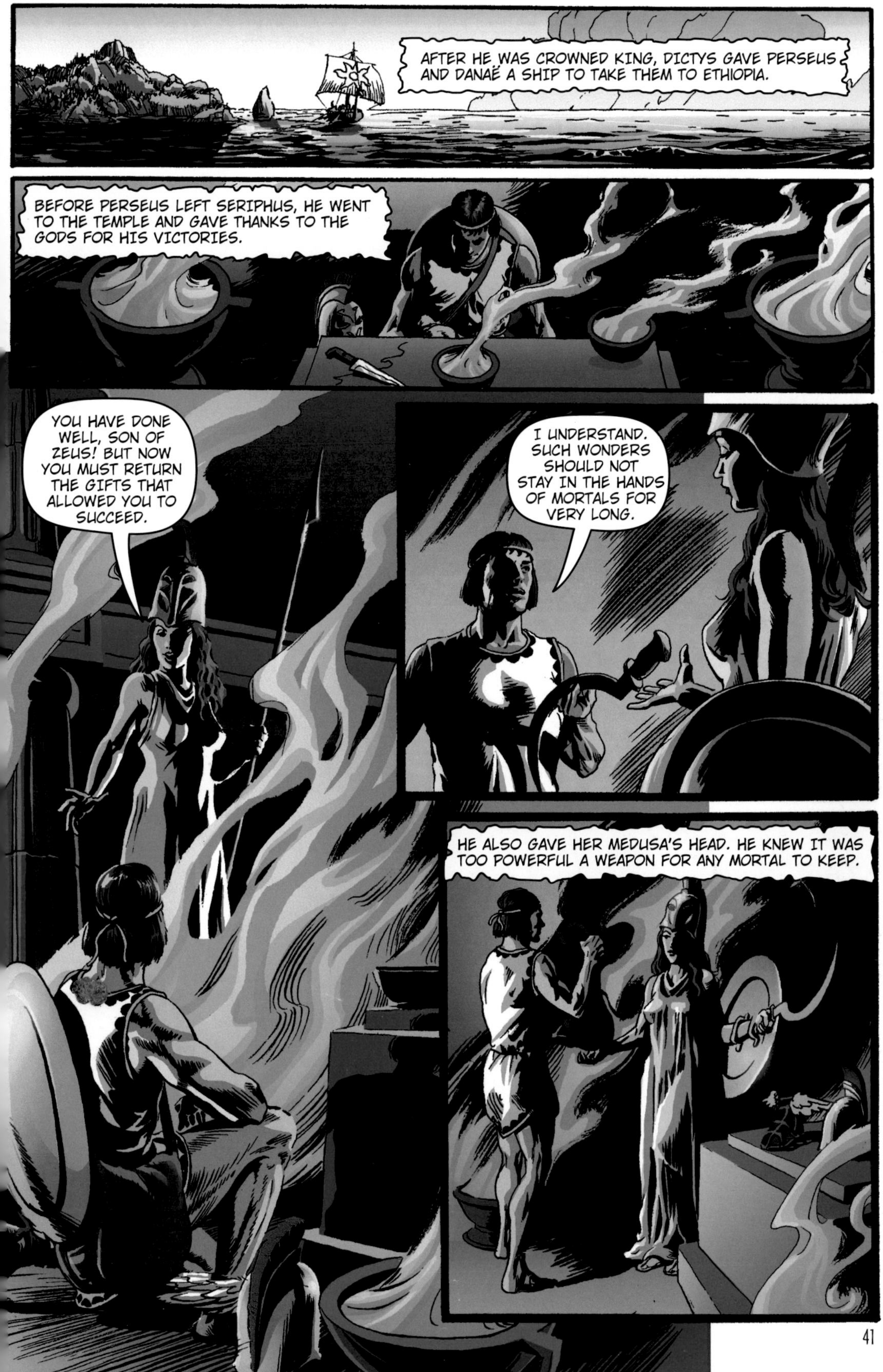
AFTER HE WAS CROWNED KING, DICTYS GAVE PERSEUS AND DANAË A SHIP TO TAKE THEM TO ETHIOPIA.
BEFORE PERSEUS LEFT SERIPHUS, HE WENT TO THE TEMPLE AND GAVE THANKS TO THE GODS FOR HIS VICTORIES.
YOU HAVE DONE WELL, SON OF ZEUS! BUT NOW YOU MUST RETURN THE GIFTS THAT ALLOWED YOU TO SUCCEED.
I UNDERSTAND. SUCH WONDERS SHOULD NOT STAY IN THE HANDS OF MORTALS FOR VERY LONG.
HE ALSO GAVE HER MEDUSA'S HEAD. HE KNEW IT WAS TOO POWERFUL A WEAPON FOR ANY MORTAL TO KEEP.

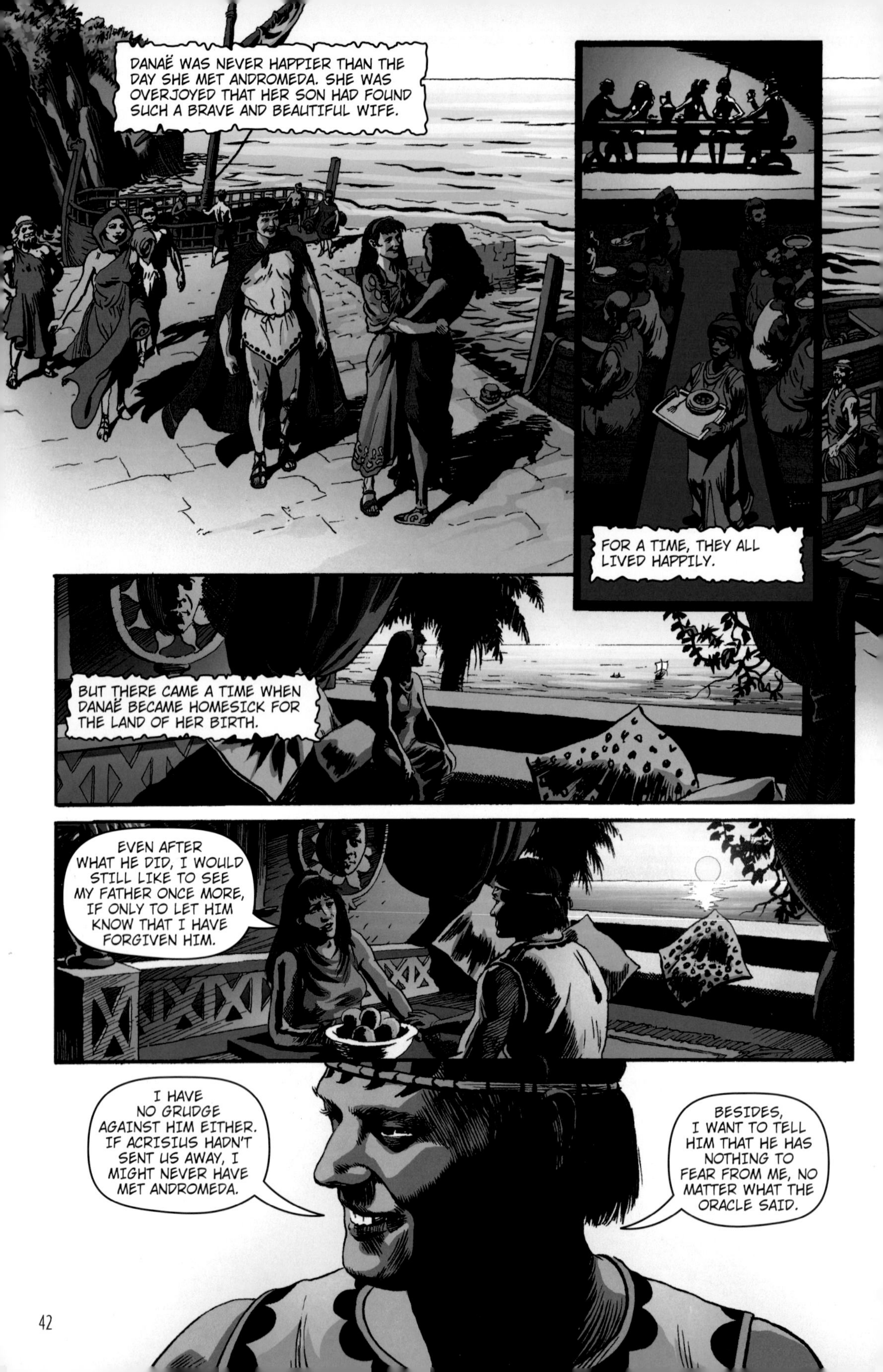
DANAË WAS NEVER HAPPIER THAN THE DAY SHE MET ANDROMEDA. SHE WAS OVERJOYED THAT HER SON HAD FOUND SUCH A BRAVE AND BEAUTIFUL WIFE.
FOR A TIME, THEY ALL LIVED HAPPILY.
BUT THERE CAME A TIME WHEN DANAË BECAME HOMESICK FOR THE LAND OF HER BIRTH.
EVEN AFTER WHAT HE DID, I WOULD STILL LIKE TO SEE MY FATHER ONCE MORE, IF ONLY TO LET HIM KNOW THAT I HAVE FORGIVEN HIM.
I HAVE NO GRUDGE AGAINST HIM EITHER. IF ACRISIUS HADN'T SENT US AWAY, I MIGHT NEVER HAVE MET ANDROMEDA.
BESIDES, I WANT TO TELL HIM THAT HE HAS NOTHING TO FEAR FROM ME, NO MATTER WHAT THE ORACLE SAID.

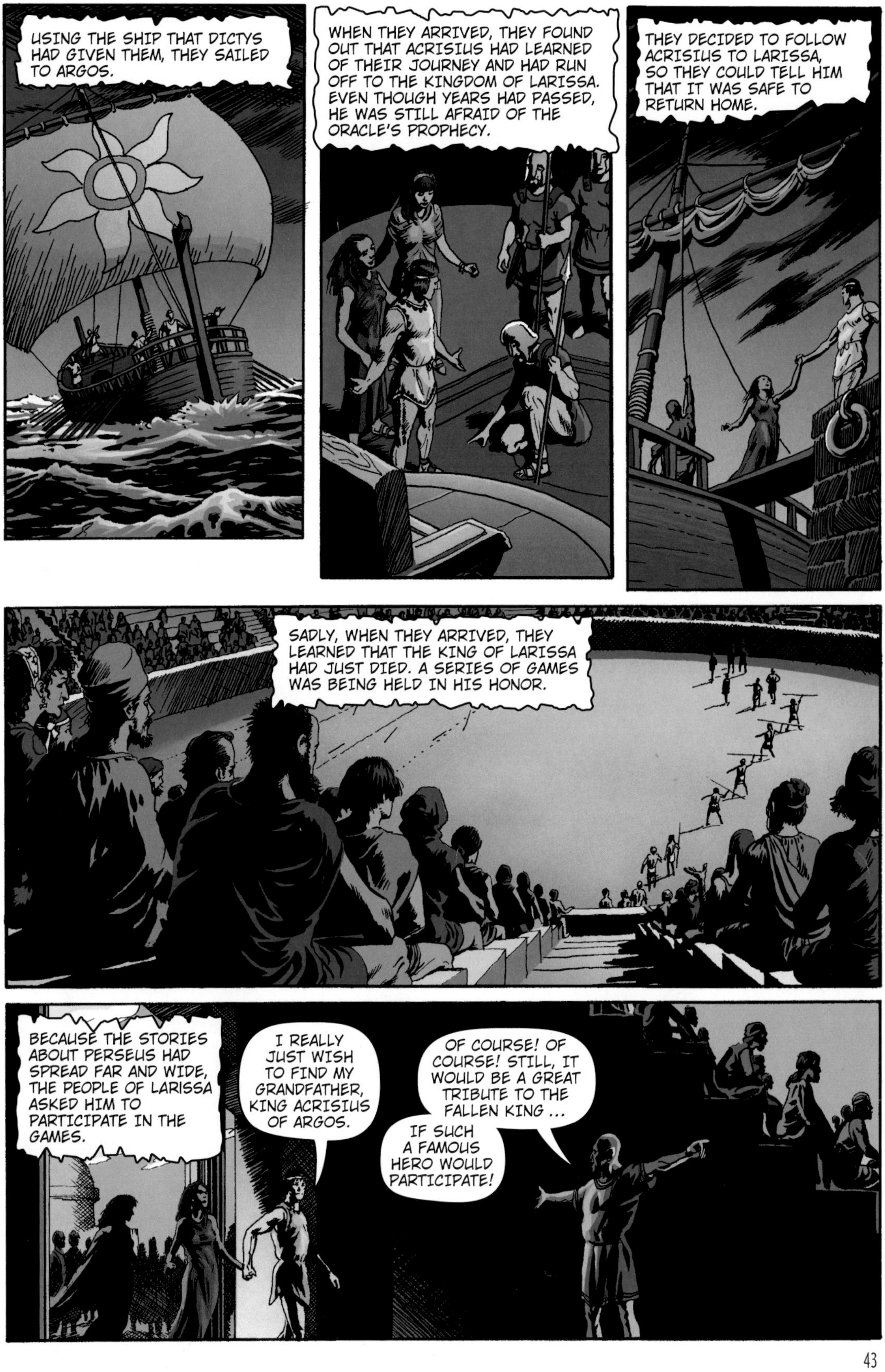
USING THE SHIP THAT DICTYS HAD GIVEN THEM, THEY SAILED TO ARGOS.
WHEN THEY ARRIVED, THEY FOUND OUT THAT ACRISIUS HAD LEARNED OF THEIR JOURNEY AND HAD RUN OFF TO THE KINGDOM OF LARISSA. EVEN THOUGH YEARS HAD PASSED, HE WAS STILL AFRAID OF THE ORACLE'S PROPHECY.
THEY DECIDED TO FOLLOW ACRISIUS TO LARISSA, SO THEY COULD TELL HIM THAT IT WAS SAFE TO RETURN HOME.
SADLY, WHEN THEY ARRIVED, THEY LEARNED THAT THE KING OF LARISSA HAD JUST DIED. A SERIES OF GAMES WAS BEING HELD IN HIS HONOR.
BECAUSE THE STORIES ABOUT PERSEUS HAD SPREAD FAR AND WIDE, THE PEOPLE OF LARISSA ASKED HIM TO PARTICIPATE IN THE GAMES.
I REALLY JUST WISH TO FIND MY GRANDFATHER, KING ACRISIUS OF ARGOS.
OF COURSE! OF COURSE! STILL, IT WOULD BE A GREAT TRIBUTE TO THE FALLEN KING ...
IF SUCH A FAMOUS HERO WOULD PARTICIPATE!

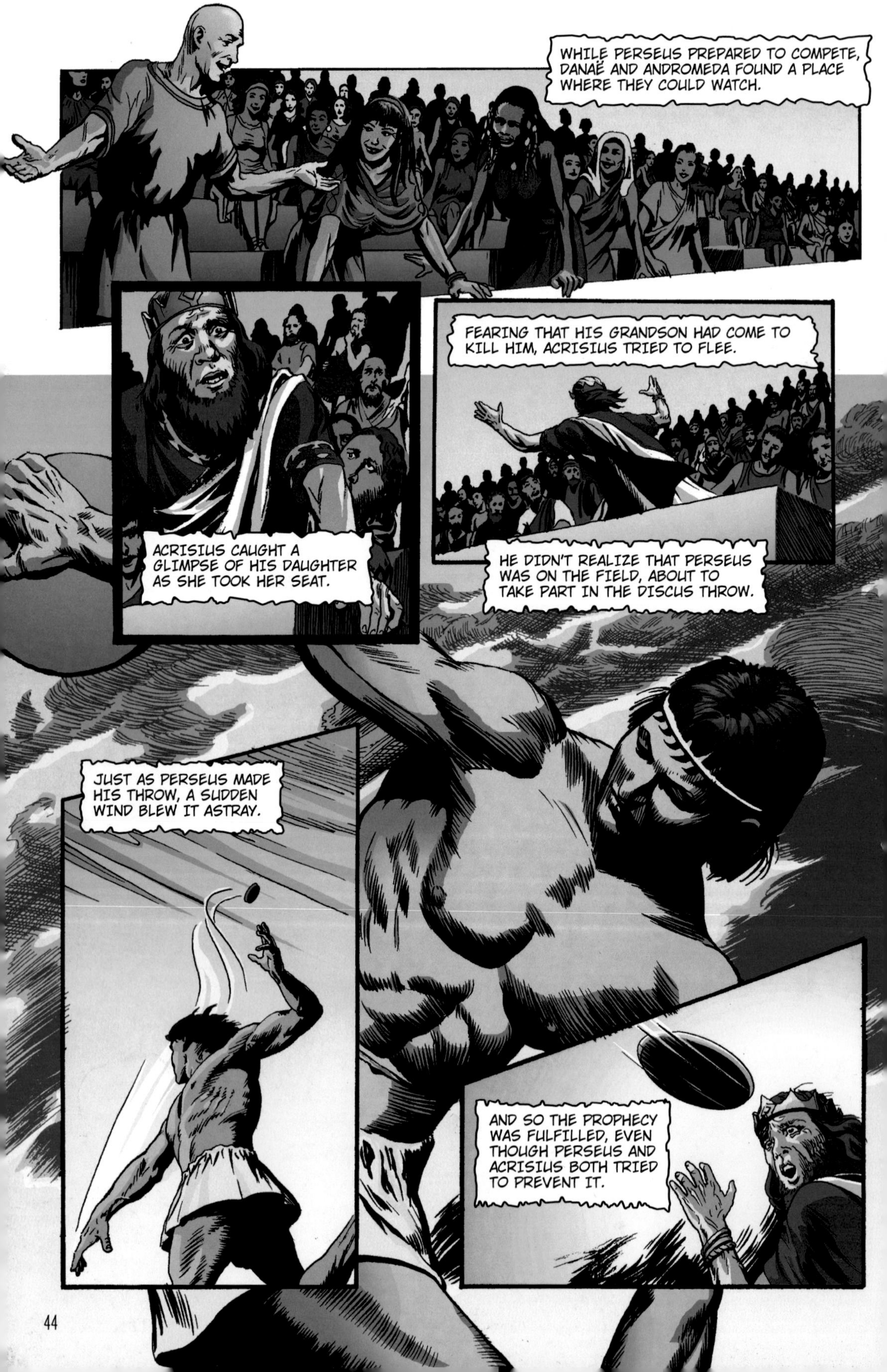
WHILE PERSEUS PREPARED TO COMPETE, DANAË AND ANDROMEDA FOUND A PLACE WHERE THEY COULD WATCH.
ACRISIUS CAUGHT A GLIMPSE OF HIS DAUGHTER AS SHE TOOK HER SEAT.
FEARING THAT HIS GRANDSON HAD COME TO KILL HIM, ACRISIUS TRIED TO FLEE.
HE DIDN'T REALIZE THAT PERSEUS WAS ON THE FIELD, ABOUT TO TAKE PART IN THE DISCUS THROW.
JUST AS PERSEUS MADE HIS THROW, A SUDDEN WIND BLEW IT ASTRAY.
AND SO THE PROPHECY WAS FULFILLED, EVEN THOUGH PERSEUS AND ACRISIUS BOTH TRIED TO PREVENT IT.

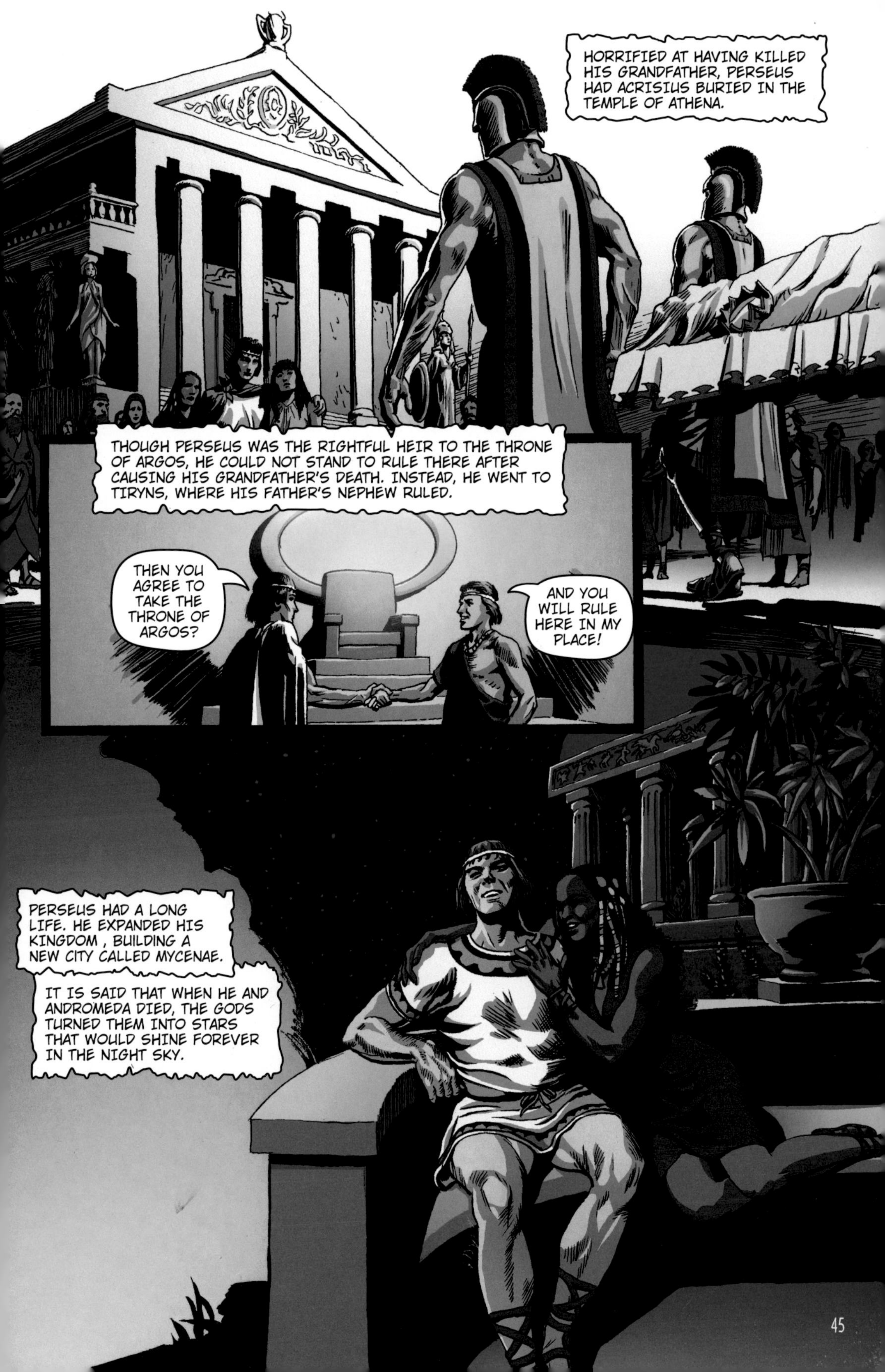
HORRIFIED AT HAVING KILLED HIS GRANDFATHER, PERSEUS HAD ACRISIUS BURIED IN THE TEMPLE OF ATHENA.
THOUGH PERSEUS WAS THE RIGHTFUL HEIR TO THE THRONE OF ARGOS, HE COULD NOT STAND TO RULE THERE AFTER CAUSING HIS GRANDFATHER'S DEATH. INSTEAD, HE WENT TO TIRYNS, WHERE HIS FATHER'S NEPHEW RULED.
THEN YOU AGREE TO TAKE THE THRONE OF ARGOS?
AND YOU WILL RULE HERE IN MY PLACE!
PERSEUS HAD A LONG LIFE. HE EXPANDED HIS KINGDOM , BUILDING A NEW CITY CALLED MYCENAE.
IT IS SAID THAT WHEN HE AND ANDROMEDA DIED, THE GODS TURNED THEM INTO STARS THAT WOULD SHINE FOREVER IN THE NIGHT SKY.

GLOSSARY AND PRONUNCIATION GUIDE

ACRISIUS (ah-*cree*-see-uhs): the King of Argos, father of Danaë, and grandfather of Perseus

ADAMANTINE (a-duh-*man*-teen): an unbreakable material

ANDROMEDA (an-*drah*-meh-deh): the princess of Ethiopia, whom Perseus rescues from the Kraken

ARGOS (*ahr*-gohs): ancient Greek city where Perseus was born

ATHENA (uh-*thee*-nuh): the Greek goddess of wisdom

CASSIOPEIA (ka-see-uh-*pee*-uh): the wife of King Cepheus and mother of Andromeda

CEPHEUS (*see*-fee-uhs): the king of Ethiopia, husband of Queen Cassiopeia, and father of Andromeda

DANAË (*da*-nah-ee): Perseus' mother

DICTYS (*dik*-tees): a fisherman, brother of King Polydectes

GRAEAE (gray-ay): the three blind witches from whom Perseus learns the location of the Gorgons

HADES (*hay*-deez): the Greek god of the underworld

HERMES (*hur*-meez): the messenger of the gods of Mount Olympus

MYCENAE (my-*see*-nee): an ancient Greek city founded by Perseus

ORACLE (*ohr*-uh-kul): in ancient Greece, a priestess or other person through whom the gods were believed to communicate

PEGASUS (*peg*-uh-sus): a winged horse that arises from the blood of the slain Medusa

PERSEUS (*purr*-see-uhs): the son of Zeus and Danaë and king of Mycenae

PHINEUS (*finn*-ee-uhs): Cepheus' kinsman, to whom Andromeda had been promised in marriage

POLYDECTES (pah-lee-*dehk*-tees): the king of Seriphus and brother of Dictys

POSEIDON (poh-*sy*-duhn): the Greek god of the sea

SERIPHUS (sah-*ree*-fuhs): a small island kingdom located in the Aegean Sea

TIRYNS (teer-inz): an ancient Greek kingdom, ruled by Perseus for many years

FURTHER READING, WEBSITES, AND MOVIES

Clash of the Titans. DVD. Directed by Desmond Davis. Hollywood, CA: Warner Brothers Entertainment, 1981. The story of Perseus' adventures is told in this classic early 1980s special effects extravaganza.

Day, Nancy. *Your Travel Guide to Ancient Greece*. Minneapolis: Twenty-First Century Books, 2001. Day prepares readers for a trip back to ancient Greece, including which cities to visit, how to get around, what to wear, and how to fit in with the locals.

Limke, Jeff. *Theseus: Battling the Minotaur*. Minneapolis: Graphic Universe, 2008. Follow the adventures of another great Greek hero in this exciting volume from the Graphic Myths and Legends series. Theseus shows he is fit to be king of Athens by defeating several enemies, including the fearsome Minotaur, a monster who is half-man, half-bull.

Mythweb. http://www.mythweb.com/index.html. This site, with a searchable encyclopedia, provides readers with information on gods, goddesses, and places in Greek myth, including information about Perseus.

Storrie, Paul. *Hercules: The Twelve Labors*. Minneapolis: Graphic Universe, 2007. Ancient Greece's greatest hero tackles his greatest challenge in this volume of the Graphic Myths and Legends series.

CREATING *PERSEUS: THE HUNT FOR MEDUSA'S HEAD*

Editor's Note: Sources conflict as to the home of Andromeda and her parents. Some say she was a princess of the ancient East African kingdom of Ethiopia—the setting chosen for this book. Others place her in the ancient city of Joppa, which is located near the modern-day city of Tel-Aviv, Israel. To retell this ancient story for modern readers, author Paul D. Storrie consulted the two classic English-language anthologies of Greek tales—*The Age of Fable* (1859) by Thomas Bulfinch and *Mythology* (1942) by Edith Hamilton. Both books are based upon the classic works of ancient poets, including Ovid and Virgil. Artist Thomas Yeates based the story's visual details on reference books on ancient Greece and East Africa, as well as photos and scenes from classic films such as *Clash of the Titans*. Special thanks to Professor David Mulroy of the University of Wisconsin-Milwaukee, who lent his expertise to ensure that the story was accurate visually and historically.

INDEX

ABOUT THE AUTHOR AND THE ARTIST

PAUL D. STORRIE was born and raised in Detroit, Michigan, and returned to live there again and again after living in other cities and states. He began writing professionally in 1987 and has written comics for Caliber Comics, Moonstone Books, Marvel Comics, and DC Comics. Some of the titles he's worked on include *Batman Beyond*, *Gotham Girls*, *Captain America: Red, White and Blue*, and *Mutant X*.

THOMAS YEATES began his art training in high school and continued at Utah State University and Sacramento State University. Subsequently, he was a member of the first class at Joe Kubert's School, a trade program for aspiring comic book artists in New Jersey. Yeates has worked as an illustrator for DC Comics, Marvel, Dark Horse, and many other companies, drawing *Tarzan*, *Zorro*, *The Swamp Thing*, *Time Spirits*, *Captain America*, and *Conan*. Yeates's many titles for the Graphic Myths and Legends series include *King Arthur: Excalibur Unsheathed*, *Arthur and Lancelot: the Fight for Camelot*, *Atalanta: the Race against Destiny*, *Robin Hood: Outlaw of Sherwood Forest*, and *Odysseus: Escaping Poseidon's Curse*.